MANAGEMENT

OF

INTERNATIONAL CONSTRUCTION

PROJECTS

Proceedings of a conference organized
by The Institution of Civil Engineers and
held in London on 14–15 November 1984

Thomas Telford, London

Conference Organizing Committee: M. H. J. Sargent (Chairman), J. B. Fisher, J. H. Armstrong, M. J. Barnett and H. W. Try

Published for the Institution of Civil Engineers by Thomas Telford Ltd, PO Box 101, 26–34 Old Street, London EC1P 1JH

First published 1985

British Library Cataloguing in Publication data

Management of international construction projects
1. Construction industry — Management
2. Industrial project management
I. Institution of Civil Engineers
624'.068'4   TH438

ISBN 0 7277 0220 3

Printed in Great Britain by Billing and Sons Ltd, Worcester.

Contents

Paper 2 was not submitted for publication and Paper 13 was
withdrawn.

1 Project finance—the multilateral development banks

D. B. MINCH, International Finance Corporation, Washington DC

The Multilateral Development Banks (MDBs) comprise four institutions - the World Bank Group, the Inter-American Development Bank, the Asian Development Bank, and the African Development Bank. The International Finance Corporation (IFC) is the arm of the World Bank Group which invests funds on a commercial basis in private sector projects in developing countries. This paper addresses the financing of international projects in the countries where the MDBs can operate and focuses on the opportunities for the private sector in the development process.

One estimate of the magnitude of the funds flowing into developing countries for capital investment is given in the following table:

Net Resource Receipts of Developing Countries
US$ billion at current prices

	1975	1980	1981	1982
MDB Disbursements	4.2	8.0	9.5	11.2
Official Development Assistance	19.9	35.9	34.8	32.2
Export Credits	5.6	13.6	13.3	11.4
Foreign Commercial Lending[1]	12.4	23.4	31.0	23.0
Direct Investment	10.5	10.5	16.1	11.0
Other[2]	4.0	4.6	3.2	4.4
Total	56.6	96.0	107.9	93.2

[1] Excluding short-term lending.
[2] Excluding IMF support.
   Source: OECD (DAC Nov. '83), and MDB Reports.

Management of international construction projects. Thomas Telford Ltd, London, 1984.

1

Complete 1983 figures are not available at the time of writing. However, it is clear from estimates that for the first time developing countries as a group received less in 1983 from new medium and long term loan disbursements than they paid to service outstanding obligations of this type. A major component in this fall in disbursements was a curtailment of foreign commercial lending.

As is apparent from the table, MDB disbursements account for a relatively small average proportion (1982: 12%) of total capital flows to developing countries; though for a number of reasons these flows are much more important than their size would suggest. For in addition to their role in providing project finance and technical assistance, the MDBs also act as financial catalysts, institution builders and policy advisors. They are influential in promoting prudent government economic policies and rational development priorities in the developing countries they serve.

Disbursement as a measurement understates the contribution the MDBs make to capital flows. IFC, for instance, frequently syndicates project financial packages which include funds from commercial banks or insurance companies, but only IFC's own funds appear statistically as MDB disbursements. The World Bank also increasingly arranges cofinancing from other sources to supplement its own capital resources. Moreover, disbursements usually fall well below the level of funds approved by the MDBs in any year, representing the lag between commitment of funds and their actual draw-down.

For instance, in the fiscal year ending June 30, 1983 the World Bank[1] alone approved US\$14.5 billion of its own funds to developing countries, most of which was project related and the following table indicates the distribution of that total by sector:

	World Bank[1] Commitments 1983 (US\$ billion)
Agriculture & rural development	3.7
Energy	2.8
Industry[2]	2.5
Transportation	1.9
Water & Sewerage	0.8
Others	2.8
Total	14.5

1/ IBRD + IDA but excl. IFC
2/ Including small scale enterprises and loans to development finance companies.
Source: World Bank Annual Report 1983.

Since the Bank generally finances only about one third of the capital cost of its projects, its influence on the financing of projects extends beyond the level of its commitments to about US\$40 billion of annual investment.

Assuming similar ratios for the other MDBs, the combined influence of the MDBs probably extends to about US$50 billion of annual capital expenditure. In terms of numbers of projects, the World Bank approved about 250 loans or credits in 1983 in the public sector, while IFC approved investments in about 60 projects in the private sector.

Public Sector Projects

In the case of the public sector, the MDBs identify potential projects in consultation with the host country, following a process of joint study aimed at agreeing investment priorities within the framework of a coherent development strategy.

After a project has been identified in this way, it enters the preparation phase, a period normally of one or two years. Though formal responsibility for project preparation rests with the host country, the MDBs often play an active role. That role has a number of objectives; for instance, to ensure that the project is conceptually adequate and complete, to help the host country find the finance and engineering assistance needed to define the project and estimate capital costs, and to ensure that the MDBs' requirements and standards are understood. A critical element in project preparation is a review of alternative technical solutions so as to select the one offering optimum cost benefit in the host country's national context, rather than, for instance, the most technically advanced.

When the project has taken shape, it is ready for appraisal. In World Bank projects, appraisal is the Bank's responsibility and it is conducted by the Bank's own staff, supplemented when required by individual external consultants. Typically the appraisal team spends several weeks in the field reviewing the technical, institutional, economic and financial aspects of the projects.

Technical appraisal is concerned with questions such as physical scale, layout, location, process, proposed contractual arrangements and implementation schedule. Institutional appraisal focuses on the implementing agency's organisation and management in the context of its ability to undertake the project and achieve its long-term objectives. Economic appraisal measures the project's contribution to the host country's economic development by applying state of the art analytical methods appropriate to the sector. Financial appraisal has several purposes; for instance, to ensure that overall funding for the project is sufficient, to review price levels for the product or services the project will provide and to measure financial viability.

On its return from the field the Bank's appraisal team prepares a report identifying the issues to be resolved, setting out its conclusions and recommending the terms and conditions of the proposed loan. Negotiations between the Bank and the borrower follow and lead to the drafting of a loan agreement, after which the project is placed before the Bank's board of directors for approval. Only when the board has approved the project and the loan agreement has been signed, are borrowers in a position to solicit formal bids from contractors and suppliers with a firm knowledge that they will be able to place contracts.

Each loan for a public sector project is made to the host government or, if made to an implementing agency, must be guaranteed by the government concerned. World Bank loans are invariably linked to the supply of specific goods or services within the project and procurement of these goods and services is carried out in accordance with guidelines.

The Bank usually requires its borrowers to obtain the designated goods or services through international competitive bidding. In cases where international competitive bidding may not be justified or appropriate, other methods of procurement are permitted by the guidelines, and the specific procedures to be adopted in each case are specified in the loan agreement which is a legally binding document. The project contractual arrangements must be compatible with the requirement that goods or services financed wholly or in part by a World Bank loan are procured in accordance with the agreed procedures. Different procurement procedures may apply to goods and services for the project which are financed exclusively from non-Bank funds.

Cofinancing with partners is an increasingly important method of augmenting the Bank's resources. Of the approximately 250 World Bank loans and credits approved during 1983 for the public sector, 88 were cofinanced projects with a total cost of US$ 21.0 billion, towards which the Bank itself committed about 28% of the funding.

The three main categories of cofinancing partners with the Bank are: (a) official development agencies, other MDBs, and funds, such as those based in oil-rich countries: (b) export credit agencies, which are directly associated with financing the procurement of certain goods and services from a particular country: and (c) commercial banks. Cofinancing for projects is feasible only when all three parties to the transaction - the borrower, the cofinanciers, and the World Bank - see advantages. But because of the variables involved, the actual arrangements and the roles of the parties vary from case to case.

For instance, some colenders have inhibitions which limit freedom of procurement, while others may be indifferent to the sourcing or method of procurement. Cofinancing on a parallel basis with agencies having procurement inhibitions requires exchange of information early in the project cycle to identify and package goods and services to suit that agency. For those public sector agencies that can borrow at least some of their capital needs on commercial terms, the most important source of additional external financing is the commercial banks. In today's international capital markets, however, commercial banks are reluctant to increase, or even maintain, earlier levels of lending to numerous developing countries.

In order to make it easier for commercial banks to join as joint colenders in World Bank projects, new financial instruments were introduced by the Bank in 1983. These were intended to make it possible for commercial banks to extend their normal loan maturities and grace periods. By providing commercial banks ways in which they can become more closely associated with the World Bank, it is hoped that their perception of the quality and security of cofinanced assets will be better and that they will correspondingly increase their levels of lending.

The effect on international contractors and suppliers of an increase in cofinancing should be twofold. Firstly, it should provide increased opportunities to bid on new projects, since Bank procurement guidelines would apply more widely. And secondly, since Bank standards will have been the criteria used for project preparation, the project management and contractual arrangements are more likely to work; and there is a reasonable probability that the project itself will achieve its objectives and provide a positive development benefit to the host country.

How do interested firms get timely intelligence about World Bank projects? Of course, contractors and suppliers maintain a direct or indirect presence in markets which interest them. They can also keep themselves informed through their embassies. However, the World Bank's Monthly Operational Summary provides regularly updated information about Bank projects from the earliest stages in the project cycle. Moreover, the Bank's Technical Data Sheets provide details, at the stage following board approval, of goods and services to be procured for projects. Both publications can be obtained from Johns Hopkins University Press, Baltimore, MD 21218, USA. Development Forum Business Edition contains general procurement notices about MDB financed projects, usually prior to board approval, and can be ordered from the UN, CH-1211 Geneva 10, Switzerland.

Private Sector Projects

There is now a general recognition that, if past growth rates in developing countries are to be restored, private investment must play a larger role. Governments have recently become more receptive to proposals from the private sector and more aware of the benefits of policies which encourage private sector activity and are finding that such incentives need not compromise the attainment of other objectives.

However, the crisis from which the world economy is emerging has had a damaging impact on private enterprise in many developing countries. Manufacturers in many developing countries have been hit during the recession by reduced demand leading to under-utilization of capacity and depressed prices for their output. Lower internal cash generation with correspondingly reduced capacity to service debt results from these conditions. In addition, in some countries the local currency value of debt contracted in foreign exchange has risen substantially as the result of drastic devaluations. At the same time, international lending by commercial banks, which had tended over the past decade to substitute excessively for direct equity investment, has slumped. Financial distress has led to increased arrears, defaults on debt repayments, reschedulings and foreclosures.

IFC, the private sector arm of the World Bank Group, has the task of encouraging and supporting development in the private sector, both by financing worthwhile new projects and by rehabilitating potentially good enterprises which have become financially distressed.

In 1983 IFC's board approved investments grossing US$845 million in 58 projects estimated to cost a total of US$2.9 billion. While the core of IFC's portfolio is represented by investments in manufacturing industry, there has been a trend in recent years towards diversification. The percentages by sector for 1983 are given in the following table:

IFC Commitments 1983

	by no. of investments	by US$ amount
	------------------------- % -------------	
Manufacturing Industry	38	57
Agribusiness	24	7
Energy and Minerals	15	26
Capital Markets	19	7
Tourism	4	3
Total	100	100

IFC's objectives, operational capabilities and catalytic role fill a gap in the activities of export credit agencies and banks on the one hand, and private sources of direct equity investment on the other. IFC's ability to invest in equity and to provide project loan finance to ventures, without seeking financial guarantees from the host government, uniquely complements the role of the MDBs.

The generation and identification of potential IFC projects is a pragmatic process. In contrast to the centrally planned approach to project identification in the public sector, most private sector projects originate as the perception of a market opportunity. The evolution of a concept into a defined project and the subsequent development of the institutional capacity to manage the enterprise requires considerable energy, will and endurance from the promoting group. There is no uniform pattern of project origin in the over 500 investments now composing IFC's portfolio, but many are businesses characterised by a foreign technical partner collaborating with a local entrepreneur in a joint venture.

The criteria by which new projects are selected by IFC for possible support are based on judgement and market principles. The limitations are, however, that IFC cannot consider a project in a member country not classified as "developing" or one whose government objects. Projects may be introduced to IFC by entrepreneurs in the host country or by potential foreign partners. They may choose any stage in the project cycle, from the conceptual to the definitive, to come and talk about it. IFC's interest in considering a particular investment opportunity then often acts as a catalyst for other institutional and private investors who would not otherwise be interested in a venture perceived to be of relatively high risk, particularly in its early stages. IFC therefore functions essentially like an investment bank with a developmental focus.

When introducing projects to IFC, sponsors often prefer an informal approach at first but at an early stage information in writing will be needed. There is no standard form of application. What IFC needs are the basic parameters of a specific project, with the rationale behind it and the identity of the proposed participants. Once they have been identified, private sector projects are processed by IFC in phases, but unlike the more deliberate pace of the public sector, the cycle progresses at a speed dictated by commercial pressures.

The first milestone which a project encounters is the formal initial evaluation. The purpose of this is to enable IFC to decide at an early stage whether or not an investment proposal merits further consideration. During its initial evaluation, IFC's staff will scrutinise the intrinsics of the project and address itself to a series of basic questions, of which the following are examples:

- Is there a market for what is to be produced?
- What are the interests of each of the parties in the project?
- Will the project's sponsors provide competent management?
- Will what is to be produced contribute positively to the economic development of the host country?
- Is the raw material source physically and financially secure?
- Does the location make sense and is a suitable site available?
- Are the proposed production processes technically appropriate and commercially proven?

7

- Is the capital cost reasonable, and where are the risks of overrun?
- Are the necessary utilities available and secure?
- Are the contractual arrangements proposed by the sponsoring group sensible and practicable?
- What equity exposure does the sponsoring group have?
- Based on reasonably conservative revenue and operating assumptions, do the key financial indicators appear likely to be in the acceptable range?
- What can be done by the project's sponsors to improve the project?

Once it has passed its initial evaluation, the project may go through a phase of further development, improvement or restructuring for which the project sponsor is responsible, though IFC may help. Technical assistance may be required by sponsoring groups during this phase and in certain circumstances IFC may be able to find appropriate interim financial support. Finally, when it has taken its definitive shape, the project is ready for appraisal.

Since IFC's investments are wholly dependent on the financial success of the venture and do not have the support of host government guarantees, their appraisal is more commercially oriented than comparable public sector projects, though no less thorough. In particular, the financial aspects tend to be more closely examined. The project financial plan should be adequate in total to complete the project, but not excessive; while its gearing should provide safe debt service coverage and acceptable current ratios. IFC's appraisal reports aim to assess the project risks, identify outstanding issues that must be resolved before the investment can be made, and measure the financial and economic rates of return to be expected. Appraisal reports are frequently made available to institutional co-investors in IFC's projects and ultimately form the basis for the board's decision to invest.

IFC makes project finance available in a number of currencies and is free to negotiate the form of its equity and loan investments on a case by case basis. The Corporation is required by its Articles of Association to "undertake its financing on terms and conditions which it considers appropriate, taking into account the requirements of the enterprise, the risks being undertaken by the Corporation and the terms and conditions normally obtained by private investors for similar financing".

Unlike the other MDBs which have strict guidelines calling for international competitive bidding as the norm for the procurement of the goods and services which they finance, IFC rarely specifies what procurement procedures should be applied, though it does encourage the creation of competitive contractual arrangements to the extent that this is commercially practicable.

In the case of plant and equipment supply, this is usually accomplished by project managers inviting proposals from internationally known suppliers rather than by formal pre-qualification and tendering processes. Civil engineering construction and plant erection tend, by contrast, to be more usually the subject of limited but formal bidding.

A common feature in industrial projects is the incorporation of special equipment or process technology which has been developed or licenced by the project's foreign technical partner and is therefore subject to secrecy or patent protection. For such procurement, it can be difficult to create a normal competitive situation; and in the absence of competition IFC applies tests with the aim of safeguarding the interests of the investors as a whole against being overcharged.

Most projects face implementation problems. In order to be aware of such problems in advance of their actual occurence, IFC monitors implementation and will urge project management to plan solutions to impending problems. Another objective of project monitoring or supervision however is to get feed-back to improve the preparation of future projects.

After implementation is complete and the enterprise has been generating revenues for some time, IFC staff prepare a completion report in which the key assumptions made during appraisal are compared with reality. Some of these findings can be sobering. An example is the comparison of project capital costs estimated at appraisal with the actual cost to complete, made with a view to identifying the areas and causes of cost overruns.

IFC's experience has been that the predominating areas of project cost overruns in industrial projects are in civil engineering and in mechanical & electrical erection, rather than, for instance, in the supply of plant and equipment. Part of this stems from the difficulty of estimating construction costs before physical quantities are known, but a contributing cause has been the increased incidence of claims from contractors.

Project sponsors have daunting long-term financial risks to face in starting new ventures and during project implementation they expect to have to bear normal owners' risks, such as those originating from force majeure. Unfortunately, main contractors have increasingly come to see themselves as providers of services where all real financial risk associated with construction is transferred either to less privileged subcontractors or, more usually, to the owner. Once they are installed, main contractors are often in a position to claim additional payments on some contractual pretext as a condition of maintaining the project implementation programme. Owners are then caught between negotiating, or of seeing completion delayed; the cost of which, at a time of high real interest rates, can be devastating to their financial return.

In an effort to avoid the claims, delays and cost overruns which threaten projects, some sponsors have considered alternative construction methods. One alternative which is sometimes practicable, is the prefabrication of complete process plants in shipyards. Modern yards are very well equipped to undertake chemical plant construction, have skilled work forces, and are often hungry for work. They frequently can offer project finance in the form of export credits and, moreover, are accustomed to shipbuilding contract terms where fixed prices and firm delivery dates are the norm.

IFC has an investment in a 120,000 mt/year polyethylene plant which is barge-mounted. The barge-mounted plant was procured in Japan and delivered on site for a fixed price 19 months after the order was placed. Both owner and shipyard benefitted. The owner avoided cost overruns and was in possession of the plant ahead of schedule, while the yard earned a bonus for its efforts.

The Industrial Joint Venture

The joint venture is one of the more effective vehicles for overseas development in the private sector. Its usual purposes are to reduce the risk of failure below what it would be if one of the participants were to proceed alone and to provide a politically acceptable corporate structure for the enterprise. Moreover, the combination of participants' strengths usually exceeds the sum of the individual parts. The normal type of joint venture in developing countries is that between foreign and local participants.

Of course, joint ventures can be set up on an ad hoc basis, without incorporation, where the objective is limited; for instance, by a foreign contractor with a local counterpart to undertake a public works contract, or by agencies to market a product. However, it is the incorporated joint venture which can have its own capital structure and borrowing capacity which is of more developmental interest. An analysis of multi-national companies' foreign direct investment[1] provides an insight into the motives large companies have for their investments in developing countries.

Their dominant motives are seen as the need to gain access to the host country's domestic market and to avoid or preempt tariff barriers, though avoiding nontariff barriers to trade had become a more important motive by 1983. "Tax advantages" and "inducements offered by the host country" were regarded as relatively unimportant, though some companies stressed that specific inducements could, on occasion, tip the balance. Contrary to widespread impression, most multi-national companies do not appear to be greatly influenced by access to "cheap labor" or "cheap raw materials".

---

[1] Foreign Direct Investment 1973-87 published by The Group of Thirty, New York, 1984.

Comparative labor cost advantages were not mentioned by high technology industries, chemical companies, food and drink companies, electrical companies or pharmaceutical companies. These were not a consideration even for those companies making labor-intensive, low value-added bulk products for the retail trade (such as soap, detergents, surgical dressings etc.).

Often these companies had production facilities in dozens of countries. But the dominant consideration, again, was whether the local market could support an economical level of production. In most cases the use of developing countries as an export base was not particularly attractive to multi-nationals though there were exceptions to this in certain specific industries.

Clearly, developing countries cannot depend on multi-national companies as the main source of private sector projects. Smaller and more specialised companies have an important role to play and professional engineers associated with suppliers, contractors and consultants can help to stimulate and encourage the development process by contributing the ideas from which projects originate. The joint venture can then provide the vehicle for spreading the burden of project promotion and for reducing the financial risks involved.

A foreign promoter should take great care in choosing a local participant in the host country, whose interests are complementary, perhaps to obtain technical know-how, a management input, or even an export market. Both partners bring intangible benefits to the joint venture. The local participant may bring influence and knowledge of how to get things done effectively in the local environment. The foreign partner may bring credibility without which financial support for the project could not be obtained. It is important, however, that the participants should agree at an early stage what their objectives are.

A study of past failures can provide useful information for those contemplating joint venture initiatives. One major cause of joint venture failure is lack of goal congruence between the foreign and local participants, whether caused by misunderstanding of intentions or inadequate communication.

Such failures usually exhibit themselves early in terms of personal conflict and breakdown in trust. Invariably differences exist in the culture and custom of doing business between the foreign and the local participant; and these differences may be intensified by the legal and operational framework within which a joint venture has to operate. Differences may be subordinated if the joint venture enjoys early financial success; but as soon as profitability declines the problems surface, resulting in mistrust and ultimately in a high probability of failure.

The following table contrasts some of the features of unsuccessful and successful joint ventures:

Unsuccessful Joint Venture

Foreign Partner wants:	Local Partner wants:	Host Government offers:
long term profit	quick cash returns	poorly developed
growth of business	multiple business diversifications	company laws
good quality control standards	high output	constantly changing fiscal rules
professional management	to obtain know-how so as to go it alone	ambiguous im-
employee loyalty	as soon as possible	port regu- lations
to maintain secrets	speedy (haphazard) decisions	
	management jobs for family	

Probable Result: conflict – distrust – failure.

Successful Joint Venture

Agreement on joint venture objectives
Agreement on profit distribution strategy
Agreement on reinvestment of profits
Agreement on management roles
Agreement on technology & secrecy

Probable Result: congruence – cooperation – success.

Perhaps the construction industry will see advantages in establishing joint ventures with their counterparts in developing countries of more permanence than the associations of temporary convenience which are formed to prequalify for large contracts. The construction industry after all is a major direct contributor to the process of development and over 40% of the total cost of World Bank projects goes for construction work. However, most developing countries can no longer afford to employ foreign contractors in the manner and to the extent that they did in the 1960s and 70s when the emphasis was on large basic infrastructure projects. Instead, they would like to improve their own construction capabilities to handle both new construction and maintenance work more efficiently. IFC is doing some pioneering work in this area by assisting in the establishment of a guarantee facility for bonding Turkish contractors working abroad. But contractors in developing countries often have serious management and technical shortcomings, which can be corrected in the short-term only by providing experienced technical supervisors from more advanced organisations in the same industry.

Insuring International Investment

Insurance can reduce the risk of investment in developing countries. Twenty-two capital-exporting countries, including almost all OECD countries, as well as India and the Republic of Korea, have set up national investment insurance schemes. They offer insurance of new investments against noncommercial risks abroad to nationals or residents of the insuring country.

Eligible investments have generally included equity and quasi-equity; the definition of investments extends increasingly to nonequity transactions such as profit or production-sharing arrangements, for instance, in mining or energy ventures. In general, coverage is available for three types of political risk: expropriation, currency inconvertibility, and war. Periods of insurance tend to range between fifteen and twenty years. While a few schemes offer separate coverage for individual types of political risks, most of them provide only for blanket coverage of all risks at a flat premium. Premium rates vary among the schemes, but flat premiums tend to range between 0.5 percent and 1.5 percent a year of the insured amount.

As a rule, only investments flowing into developing countries are eligible. Whereas only one scheme explicitly requires the existence of a bilateral agreement with the host country as a precondition for insuring an investment, many schemes strive to safeguard their exposure through general bilateral investment protection agreements between home and host countries.

Assistance to the development of the host country by encouraging inward investments, promotion of the home country's exports or its access to raw materials, as well as promotion of mutually advantageous economic relations, are basic objectives of the national schemes. While some schemes concentrate on one or more of these targets, others strive, with varying priorities, to integrate all of them. All schemes operate under the auspices of their respective governments. Most are required, or at least expected, to operate on a self-sustaining financial basis.

According to OECD estimates, as of December 1981 the share of total OECD investment in developing countries covered by national investment insurance averaged about 10 percent. The ability of investors to obtain national investment insurance in a particular case may be subject to constraints caused by:

-   overconcentration of risk;
-   country or investment size ceilings
-   country related policy considerations
-   inability to cover all participants in
    international joint ventures equally.

Since the early 1970s private insurance underwriters have been willing to write policies to cover noncommercial risks for firms investing in developing countries, and in the past ten years their capacity has increased significantly. Private insurers have been successful mainly by designing their schemes to complement rather than compete with national schemes, and they offer coverage that cannot be obtained elsewhere.
Insurance will not of course cover the commercial failure of a venture but can greatly reduce some of the other risks perceived by potential investors in developing countries.

Conclusion.
The main business of the MDBs as a group is financing worthwhile development projects. The regional MDBs have project processing procedures similar to the World Bank's and are oriented towards public sector transactions. With declining levels of aid and pressure on their budgets many governments are now interested in enlarging the role of the private sector in the development process. This presents new opportunities for firms in industrial countries to collaborate with entrepreneurs in developing countries. The constraint today in this process is not the availability of project finance, but the ability to generate worthwhile projects. Many of the projects financed by IFC in the past have originated as ideas in the minds of innovative individuals and been methodically developed into a defined project. Your engineering knowledge and international experience places you in a key position to initiate private sector development in this way.

3 Risk analysis and allocation

A. J. SOUTH, Willis Faber (Construction) Ltd, London

SYNOPSIS. Risk allocation in major projects, and its subsequent distribution, is often a random and ill-managed affair.

Many of the residual exposures find their way evenutally to the insurance market but more often than not the coverage afforded is insufficient, technically difficult to understand and too diffuse in its application to fulfil the true value required of it.

The answer, as always, lies with the consumer but can the insurance market be expected to change its thinking.

RISK ANALYSIS AND ALLOCATION

I am conscious of the difficulties in dealing with such a vast and complex theme in a space of only twenty minutes. The topic alone could profitably be the subject for a full day seminar. The first concern of any paper, if it properly addresses itself to this topic is the transfer of uncertainty and the price to be paid for such a transfer.

It is clear that the demand for transfer of risk is determined by a variety of key factors. It is my view that the most important single factor in the complex business of risk allocation is the inbuilt prejudices and risk attitudes of the parties involved. The risks seen by a contractor will obviously differ from the self-same risks seen through the eyes of an employer. Risk attitudes tend to get institutionalised and hence fossilised. It is clear that the corporate attitude to risk of a company like Shell would differ markedly from that of say the ruler of Dubai. Risks vary continuously throughout the project and risk perception will shift from viewpoint to viewpoint as the project progresses.

Management of international construction projects. Thomas Telford Ltd, London, 1984. 15

Insurance has a valuable role to play in the whole procedure. The risk attitudes of an owner could be substantially influenced by the knowledge that his project is protected under a ten year guarantee insurance after completion. Similarly the approach of an engineer might differ if he is aware that his professional indemnity exposure is limited to the fees he earns on that project. A contractor will view claims for acceleration or disruption through different eyes depending on the extent to which the delay risk is adequately protected by insurance. I believe it is not widely enough appreciated that a simple policy exclusion becomes a conscious decision to remove security from the party immediately affected. Similarly, a policy deductible must be funded and paid for. Policy limits represent the finite boundary of a loss area and one is entitled to ask the question what lies beyond such limits. Insurance can therefore be described as the melting pot of the risk allocation procedure.

Above all, risk allocation is part of the continuous process of communication. Poor communications in any project are usually caused by the involvement of many different disciplines, lack of attention to detail, insufficient pre-planning and sometimes, yes, fear.

What makes attitudes vary? Financial and legal pressures figure highly but for many key individuals associated with the project, such intangibles as pride and reputation come into play; both infinitely more valuable than mere money. Theoretically a scheme can be devised whereby the major risks are shared amicably, clearly and cost effectively between the four main parties concerned, the owner, the engineer, the contractor and the financier. But in practice the real world intrudes into this idyllic senario:-

For example:

The owner is a government agency politically appointed to develop a key resource of an emergent nation. The engineer who did the feasibility study has been replaced. The contractor has pared his costs to the minimum. The financier is the national state bank. The nominated insurance company is the central monopoly national insurance corporation. The insurance clauses were lifted lock stock and barrel from an earlier unrelated job in another part of the world.

Although much has been talked about the way of devising an equitable risk sharing formula, there is a considerable reluctance to discuss the complex events that require such a formula. The constraints are formidable - what is meat for the owner's cost strategy is poison for the contractor's balance sheet. In a quite literal sense the environment in which any project has to function is in practice often chaotic. The political and economic circumstances in play at any one time may be incalculable. The project team must have its own set of criteria and objectives. The objectives of an owner are to have his project constructed on time, on original budget and with an agreed performance function. The problems inherent in a complicated major project coupled with the tensions brought about by interlinking finance, government agencies, and banks with the often hostile world economy are the background against which we must all work.

Contracts, it appears to me, exist primarily because of two fundamental paradoxes, firstly that a contractor performs works on credit and secondly, that the ultimate product is worthless unless and until completed. Adversarial contractual relationships can impose considerable constraints on both parties as regards economy, speed and quality of construction. The legal system is not the ideal forum for the resolution of major disputes. I have heard it said that 80% of all the proceeds from professional imdenmity insurance policies end up in the lawyers' pockets.

No contractual arrangements are ever perfect and it is pointless to expect them to be. It is not realistic to contemplate a contract giving expression to all likely events or to the changing and inconsistent relationships between the parties and their respective risk attitudes.

Contract documents and agreements must explain the responsibilities of each party to each other and the manner, extent and form in which insurance protection will be procured and operated. If, as is often the case these days, the owner procures the cover and pays the premium then realistic arrangements must be made for the funding of the deductible and the treatment of excluded losses. Who is to take care of financial loss suffered by the owner for risks that fall outside wrapup insurance? At which point in time should the owner sit down and talk this through with his consultants? Only the owner can best spread the risks and indeed only the owner achieves optimum benefit by so doing.

An eminent loss adjuster once advanced the idea that a contract works policy was rather more a liability policy than a policy of property insurance. At the front of his mind no doubt was the applicability or otherwise of the commerciality of the original contract for the works to the measure of loss arising as a result of a claim on the policy. Preliminary costs, overhead profit, remedial works, materials and equipment provided by the employer as free issue - all these questions recur with monotonous regularity in the complex business of claims adjustment. Under the present system, apportionment and transfer of risk or liability is achieved by the use of indemnity clauses, obligation/responsibility clauses and insurance clauses. Such clauses merely shift the financial consequences of legal liability and do not alter it.

An insurance market exists, either in whole or in part for the following risks:- delayed completion, political risks, resource risks, bonding risks, design risks, testing and commissioning risks, pollution, penalties/liquidated damages insurance, performance guarantee risks, errors and omissions risks. Collectively these risks and the insurance market's flexibility in carrying them provide the lubrication between the differing contractual interests, which vary, overlap and even oppose each other. The art is in synchronising a common view that is seen as valid throughout the period of the contract. Without planning, a risk scenario can easily encompass the following unhappy circumstances. The Contractors All Risks policy will exclude defective workmanship, with no cover for the defective part. The design risk will be covered by a legal liability policy in respect of negligence only. No performance bond will be issued. Losses following delay and/or dislocation will not be covered. Deductibles will apply to a policy to suit the contractor and will be incommensurate with the total values at risk.

It is time to say a few words about the way we in the insurance market perceive these risks. Primarily the Insurance world deals with events rather than circumstances. Risks vary in probability between the absolutely predictable and totally random. They vary in severity from nuisance value, through the comfortably manageable, to the outright catastrophic. Most insurance men, at least those with a Lloyd's background would by and large echo the views of a very eminent Lloyd's Underwriter who said "I believe that I am there to consider anything offered for insurance by a broker. I look at these offerings on the basis that there is a price for everything other than a moral hazard. Judgement and selection are the overriding skills that we try to employ". I think it is true to say that in the insurance market boundaries are being pushed back if not daily then certainly year by year. Previously uninsurable exposures are now regarded as common-place. Think for example of the risk to the insurance market posed by space satellites. Markets are now emerging in the United States that are prepared to consider such exposures as resource guarantee whereby if a project founders because the raw material is not forthcoming as anticipated the policy will respond.

To the banker the main needs for protection in project finance appear to lie in the cost overrun and delay areas. The performance or execution risk is also a source of concern. However many non-recourse projects at the moment are funded by lengthy 10 year take and pay contracts and very often these are awarded to those consortia or companies or countries that not only can put together a complex and flexible financial package but also can so organise their affairs that they derive domestic profit out of an overseas supply contract. That is to say, they have the ability to bid low on a lump sum basis and then make up for that by shrewdly priced offtake agreements, particularly in strategic goods. This enables them to make apparent concessions on the contract itself, so that by the end of the day the document is largely optical. You will doubtless remember the Camell Laird story in Singapore whereby a Japanese consortium was able to guarantee an exchange rate through the year 1990. It is such examples of innovative financial planning on a hitherto unimagined scale that will set the trends in future.

One of the main problems my own industry faces is that we tend to divide ourselves into narrow specialist areas. Yet the risks and exposures flowing from major projects and their financing do not divide themselves into such neat bundles. Theoretically the large insurance companies and reinsurance companies do have the ability to insure projects from cradle to grave but such is the sophistication of insurance procurement these days that it seldom makes sense to construct such a package deal because market forces render the unbundling of such services more economic.

I would now ask you to listen to another quotation, this time from Mr Baruch Berliner in his book Limits of Insurability of Risks. "A person requiring an object of value for which cover is an absolute necessity must be aware that insurance premiums belong to the maintenance costs of the object. He is imposing on himself a risk which it costs money to cover. If the money for this is

not available then it would not be advisable to buy the
object in the first place. We can also say that the
object of value is outside the subjective limits of
insurability of the individual and that the money
available for the required cover is not sufficient to
bring the object within the area of insurability of the
risk carrier which is why purchase of the object is not
advisable." In other words, if you can't afford the
insurance, you can't afford the object to be insured.

It seems to me that the insurance market must parade its
skills more effectively, achieve better communication and
generally organise itself in such a way that the true
needs of its customers are measured more accurately, and
funded with greater flexibility and flair.

The age of the onestop financial hypermarket is, after
all, now upon us and multi-disciplinary financial
institutions are a familiar feature of Wall Street - if
not yet - the City of London.

Can it be that Insurers are selling the wrong product at
the wrong price? Or are we simply "sent the wrong way"
by you, our clients? Are you as aware as you should be
of the contribution the insurance world can make to
project risk? And are we as attuned to your needs as we
might be?

Would it not be possible for you to urge both Owner and
Contractor to sit down together and identify all the risk
exposures involved with a project? With your own unique
skills you could help them both plot a course through the
minefield of transferable risk; quantify and mark the
various constituent elements such as physical damage,
delay, market, labour, political and currency.

Why land a Contractor for 10% of a contract when his
failure at one point in time could cost the Owner 50% of
his project and yet failure at another point in time
could be relatively harmless? Why make liquidated
damages an issue, when the delay risk, properly analysed,
might be an insurable proposition?

The traditional well tested risk bearing pattern, basic
to FIDIC, has proved itself over the years and is common
currency throughout the world.

But FIDIC by common consent offers no way out of the
owner/contractor conflict of interest problem.
Conceptually, it seems to me, risk can only be allocated,
as opposed to imposed, within a non adversarial context.

20

At the end of the FIDIC Project Insurance Seminar nearly six years ago, Mr Max Abrahamson summed up the proceedings in the following way:-

"The area of risk clarification is extraordinarily difficult. It is an area of economics. It is an area of morality. It is an area of practicality. It is an area almost of philosophy and political philosophy."

I think these words are well worth re-examining today.

Economics dictate the basic pattern of risk exposures but it would be naive to imagine that the moral issues can be discounted or that the real practical world - the facts of commercial life - can be ignored.

This at any rate seems to be the conclusion of an Engineering Foundation conference in Santa Barbara California in August last year, organised by the American Society of Civil Engineers. The conference recommended, inter alia:

"The insurance industry should develop and market, an all-purpose risk policy to cover all members of a project team through the design, construction and occupancy of a building. Such umbrella coverage could help restore cooperation and teamwork on projects by removing some of the legal friction that now exists between the different professionals responsible for a project."

Let me leave you with a final thought. The owner does not bear all the residual ˙risks associated with a project. Neither can he be said to pay for the project insurances, either directly or indirectly. Any project ultimately has an end user and that end user is invariably you or me or the tax payer at large. The community thus ends up with the responsibility of funding the exposures, liability and losses associated with giant projects.

The financial community must play its part in ensuring that any such residual, uninsured risks do represent the most acceptable end of the risk spectrum and that every effort has been made to grapple with them in a realistic way before passing them on. The motto of the insurance industry should be the buck stops here.

4 Project cost control

M. O. COATES, Gardiner and Theobald, London

SYNOPSIS. The stages of cost control are traced through
the course of a project in chronological order from the
critical initial budget advice, through pre-contract
cost monitoring, to the difficult task of providing
forecast advice throughout the construction stage. The
related subjects of cash-flow forecasting, fixed and
fluctuating price tenders and settlement of final account
'claims' are discussed.

Introduction

1.   In any treatise on as broad a subject as project cost
control, it is necessary to set down guidelines. For, if
nothing else, cost control is the longest running discipline
applied to any project, for it does - or should - commence
simultaneously with the design process and lasts until the
designers and constructors are long gone and the figures
are still being counted. So in order to avoid it becoming
amorphous, the concept of this paper is set out below:-

(i)   It is written from the viewpoint of an
independent professional cost consultant
who prefers to be called in by a client at
the very initial conception of a project
and seeks to exercise cost control disclipline
at all stages thereafter.

(ii) It refers to the cost control of capital
construction projects and not to such all-
embracing topics as life-cycle costing, etc.

(iii) It will review cost control disciplines
in chronological order from the initiation
to the finalisation of a project.

(iv) In the context of the above, the paper
is divided into headings as follows:-

a.   Pre-contract project estimating

b.   Budgetary advice to clients

c.   Cash flow forecasting/monitoring

Management of international construction projects. Thomas Telford Ltd, London, 1984.

(iv) d. Cost control of variations and programme changes

         e. Fixed price and fluctuations contracts

         f. Final account claims

Pre-Contract Project Estimating

2.   It is a requirement of all but a very few client organisations that cost discipline is introduced and exercised from the very early stages. Any project, no matter how large or small, is a function of the interplay in the eternal triangle of brief, projected design and projected cost, with each being constantly tailored because of the interaction of the other two.

3.   One of the greatest problems in the entire cost control cycle comes at the very earliest stages, and it affects the first budget figures which ever see the light of day. For normally the criticality of these figures is in inverse proportion to the quality of information on which they are based. Once issued, on no matter what basis, those first figures form the marker on which all subsequent figures are based, and again, no matter how inaccurate, these are the figures which are lodged in the minds of the participants.

4.   Therefore every effort must be made to establish as careful and as reasoned a base as possible, and then to underline for all concerned its provenance.

5.   Examples of bases for initial budget figures are as follows:-

    (i) An absolute cost limit imposed by the client, so that cost becomes the dominant feature in the brief/design/cost relationship, and all decisions stem from this.

   (ii) Availability of recent and relevant experience and cost information of equivalent projects.

 (iii) Empirical yardsticks drawn from general cost information sources including such as costs per square or cubic metre for structures, and specialist yardsticks such as cost per bed for hotel and hostel accommodation, cost per inhabitant for housing, etc.

  (iv) Design information as available.

---

6.   It would, of course, be ideal if all initial budgets could be based on item (iv) - design information - but so often it is not available or only in the most outline of

forms. Therefore, great use is made of items (ii) and (iii)
at the earliest stages and these can be such a snare and
delusion. For a plateau of cost is established by the use
of them, and thereafter it is often not understood if this
is exceeded, although the particular circumstances which
subsequently emerge may have made any early judgment quite
irrelevant.

7.   For the purposes of these initial cost studies it
is of course essential to keep up to date all sources of
cost information in a form which is both cogent and ready
for retrieval. Computer storage facilities are assisting
greatly in this task. It is to be expected that any cost
consultant will have wide access to cost information in
the market indigenous to him. It becomes much more
interesting when he is working internationally and particularly when he is entering new markets overseas. Bases of
building cost are recorded in only very rudimentary form
in most countries, even including some of the most
sophisticated: there are very few countries in which cost
recording techniques are as widespread as in the United
Kingdom. Surprisingly, however, experience has shown that
it never takes very long to lay down contacts and establish
the framework of building cost in a new country to anyone
trained in the disciplines of cost planning and cost control.
Adaptation and flexibility are essential but all the
techniques are still available and still apply.

8.   It is imperative from the point of view of worthwhile cost control to move as soon as possible from early
cost information given on any sort of empirical basis to
the careful and proper cost estimating process based upon
project design information. The sooner this is done, the
more easy it is to expunge any previous figures, and
maximum opportunity should be made particularly of drawn
information, and detailed measurement and pricing put in
hand at the earliest opportunity.

9.   The United Kingdom is very fortunate in terms of
cost estimating and control in that a most valuable by-
product of its traditional system of tendering and pricing
by means of quantifying construction work is the availability of all of this pricing data for application on other
relevant cases. It does mean that the great majority of
estimates for routine construction work are produced to very
great degrees of accuracy. It has led to cost-planning
techniques of great sophistication so that very detailed
analyses for building structures can be prepared and the
effect of even the smallest change at the design stage can
be monitored through to the construction budget. It
provides the platform for cost control techniques throughout
the entire course of a project so that, even though the
information given to a client may at times be unpalatable
to him, full and due warning of the effect of all design

changes is always available.

10.   In countries where such a cost data bank is not available, it is less easy to work to such levels of accuracy. The measurement techniques are always available but the pricing thereof is difficult and may lead to adaptations and compromises which put the target at longer range. Not least a knowledge and feel of the market is essential, both nationally and more particularly internationally. Location, timing, size and type of project can have a dramatic effect on the level of pricing for the same construction operation. Contracts such as in the Falkland Islands, Diego Garcia and the early mega-projects in the Middle East would have a pricing level applied to them reflecting "building on the moon" type operations. But to have applied such levels to the smaller jobs in the Middle East initially - and latterly the larger jobs - would have represented a gross overpricing, for an indigenous market has now grown up based upon local and Third World contractors which has brought prices right down compared with early levels.

11.   The concluding advice drawn from this section referring to the critical stage of pre-contract project estimating is as follows:-

(i)   Assemble and keep up-to-date as full a cost data bank as possible.

(ii)   Use empirical "yardstick" figures only with the greatest care and with the fullest explanation.

(iii) Move as soon as possible to a proper measured estimate based upon the fullest use of design information.

(iv)   Always consider the relevant market and market forces when preparing budget information.

Budgetary Advice to Clients

12.   Once budget information is prepared, at any stage of a project, it is imperative that it is placed in full context. There is very great advantage in a client and a design team being fully aware of the status and content of all estimates. The extent of this will change through the course of the pre-contract stage and become much more detailed as design develops. At the later stages, there is nothing wrong with revealing the full scope of pricing levels, standards assumed and provisional and contingency allowances included. A full cost plan should be a working tool, to assist the client to fulfil his brief and to treat sympathetically with the problems of the designers.

13.   Client organisations have many and varied ways of working and different priorities but a check list of items to be included for consideration in any cost report to a client would include the following:-

(i)   Information on which the report is based.

(ii)   Time currency of the report, i.e. does it allow or not allow for inflation up to a start on site? Is a start date known? Does it allow for inflation through the construction period? Is the construction period known?

(iii)   Do the figures include allowance for any of the following (or are they excluded but listed as such so that the client can make separate allowances)? :-

- Cost of equipment, furnishing or other fitting-out

- Professional design team fees

- Taxes attracted by the proposed contract

- Finance during construction

- Cost of land

- Other direct costs to come out of client's budget

(iv)   Have any figures been provided from outside sources to which attention should be drawn?

(v)   Are there any special situations or caveats which could affect the figures and of which the client and the designers should be made aware?

14.   Efficient cost control should always keep abreast of the client's and the designer's thinking. Once the first full and consolidated cost plan has been prepared, it should be a process of evolution, virtually uninterrupted by the fact that a certain stage the project becomes the subject of a contract with the contractor. In the discipline of cost control, this will mean that the contract sum will be substituted for whatever had been the equivalent, estimated figure up to that time and the process continues.

15.   Therefore, in many cases of major projects, a sequence of cost reporting is established at an early stage, and moves through the pre-contract and the post-contract stages in one continuous sequence. Initially, allowances for many parts of the project may be based on quite empirical bases but these can be refined as time goes on, as well as the effect of all design changes indicated. A close and understanding working relationship between client, designers and cost consultant is, of course, essential for such cost control to be successful.

16.   Conclusions to be drawn from this section are as follows:-

    (i)   Understand your client's requirements.

    (ii) Report figures always in the fullest context.

    (iii) Keep cost control procedures up to date to reflect latest design changes.

Cash Flow Forecasting/Monitoring

17.   It is invariably the case that high on the list of any client's requirements is information on cash flow. The provision of this information represents the converse to the preparation of a cost estimate, for once the estimate has been prepared, the preparation of a cash flow presents no great problem: the difficulty comes in establishing any degree of reliability for it. Much research, both published and "in house" has been spent on this subject, and there are available typical "S" curve diagrams for expenditure on standard structures. The "S" curve will indicate a slow initial build-up of expenditure, an acceleration through the middle of the contract and a flattening-off at the end. It is on the basis of such diagrams that the majority of cash flow predictions are prepared. However, sensible consideration must again be given to the type and timing of the works being undertaken. Circumstances may suggest that standard "S" curves are inappropriate, e.g. work in existing structures may accelerate payment as compared with new: installation of major items at a late stage in any specific project may flatten out the curve initially. In the case of major projects, it may prove necessary to price the construction programme in detail to allow for the interaction of the phased completion of individual pieces of structure.

18.   The problem with cash flows is that even the most detailed and accurate forecasting exercise may not give for great accuracy, and this is on account of factors quite out of the control of the forecaster. These may include the following:-

    (i)   Acceleration or delay to the construction programme.

    (ii) Late invoicing or invoicing of materials in advance by contractors.

    (iii) Time-lag in the process of valuing work completed.

    (iv) "Up-front" payments made to contractors and sub-contractors.

    (v)   Payment withheld through defective work.

19.   The effect of all of the foregoing can mean that actual cash flow deviates quite markedly from forecasted. It is generally the case that this movement is towards decelerating payment rather than the reverse, and fortunately this is normally to the client's advantage, so no great harm is done.

20.   However, actual payment compared with forecasted cash flow is often taken as a measure of performance against contract programme and particularly so if payments are falling behind. It is, of course, reasonable that this should be the case but only to a point. Cash flow should never be taken as an absolute indicator of performance because of all the factors listed above. Nevertheless, a continuing trend of slippage of actual against forecast payment can be taken as a general if inaccurate indicator of delay to a project programme.

21.   As with the cost control procedure, cash flow monitoring should always be kept up to date. This is a simple procedure whereby actual payments can be substituted in succession for those forecasted, and the balance of payments to come is adjusted accordingly. Again in a situation of severe delay, this can be used as a broad forecasting tool so that comparative projections can be produced to indicate firstly the pattern of payments necessary if the original completion date is to be achieved (which generally is shown to be impossible): and secondly, ultimate completion date i. if forecasted rate of expenditure is achieved thereafter and ii. if actual rate of expenditure is continued. However, caution is counselled in reading too much into such figures.

22.   Concluding advice from this section is as follows:-

   (i)   Cash flows can be simply prepared for normal
         projects - often using standard "S" curve
         models.

   (ii) Major projects may require a more detailed
         pricing of programme/activity analyses.

   (iii) Cash flow forecasts cannot be regarded as
         accurate tools and are subject to various
         unforeseen factors.

   (iv) Performance against cash flow forecasts
         should only be taken as a general indicator
         of progress.

   (v)   Cash flow statements should always be
         kept up-to-date with actual payments inserted
         and adjustments made accordingly.

Cost Control of Variations and Programme Changes

23.   In the cost control cycle, a project reaches by far
the most difficult stage once it has started on site. Up
until then, the interplay of brief/design/cost is conducted
in a situation of control and there is capacity for review
and change but once construction is underway the element
of control becomes progressively weaker. For the real test
for the project and its designers now begins and new factors
come into play, which may include the following

    (i)   Unexpected site conditions.

    (ii)   Evolution of the client brief and
           development of design introducing
           variations and consequent programme
           changes.

    (iii) Capacity of third parties, including all
           types of inspection authorities, to
           introduce change to the project.

    (iv)   Delays to the construction programme
           in general terms.

24.   The aim at this stage must be to continue to
strive for cost control and not to slip back into cost
reporting. If there is true control of costs, there should
be capacity to make compensating adjustments for earlier
changes, but as the programme progresses so the ability
to do so becomes much more limited.

25.   In an ideal world, changes and consequent adjustments to contract price are a function of specific client
instruction only. In practice and particularly in the case
of major projects, this idealism becomes very clouded
between the interests and activities of client, designers,
inspecting authorities, contractors and trade unions.

26.   The great truth is that the cost controller must
keep abreast of all facets of design and site activity
and report on all of them clearly and regularly. The
normal interval for this is monthly and the categories of
cost adjustment may include the following:-

    (i)   Effect of placing orders for sub-contracts
           against previous allowances included.

    (ii)   Forecasted effect of all variations.

    (iii) Forecasted effect of placing orders or
           issuing design information against any
           provisional allowances.

    (iv)   Adjustment of remeasured values for
           sections of work so treated against
           original allowances.

(v) Anticipated result of any known future instructions not yet passed to the contractor.

(vi) Monitoring of fluctuations allowances if applicable.

(vii) Forecasted effect of any delay or acceleration to the building programme or other "claim" situations.

(viii) Identifying of further items of possible cost significance against which values cannot yet be set.

(ix) Listing of relevant items not covered by the reporting.

27.   The above represents the full spectrum which should be drawn together by the cost controller. It requires the closest working with the design team and, in the case of major projects, this means working alongside them in their offices. This is rightly a very time-consuming part of the cost consultant's role and once again it is worth reiterating that the more flexible the basis of contract pricing, the easier this makes the task of cost control. It is continuingly true that the bill of quantities, although currently under attack, still provides the best mechanism for the cost control system.

28.   The cost controller must have the courage of his convictions. It may be uncomfortable to inform a client or a design team of a worsening cost situation and to encourage sacrifices elsewhere, but it is by far a greater sin not to have done so and to have them presented with a disaster situation later when there is no hope of redress. It is never responsible cost control to set one's face against potential extra cost or "claim" situations and, although alarmism must be avoided, the earliest warning should be given, even if this means reporting in terms of high and low parameters.

29.   In conclusion, the following:-

(i) Cost control will become less effective as progress on site advances.

(ii) Nevertheless the aim must be to strive always for the earliest warning of potential cost adjustments.

(iii) Cost control reporting must be on a regular and frequent basis and must present the full spectrum of cost information.

(iv) The cost controller must have the
      courage of his convictions to give early
      warning of all cost overrun situations,
      no matter how unpalatable.

Fixed Price and Fluctuation Contracts

30.   The instinct of clients universally is to seek
fixed price contracts. This is for the obvious reason
that it removes one area of price adjustment and gives
the client that greater degree of confidence that the
tender figure and the final account will bear a close
relationship. This is particularly so in the developing
markets of the Third World where anything other than
fixed price contracts are not understood.

31.   But there are two sides to any proposition and
fixed price contracting represents a risk to contractors.
If the risk is small, they will accept it: if large, they
may not accept it or at least they will price for it. The
two principal situations when fixed price tendering may
not be sensible are firstly in the case of major projects
spanning many years and secondly when inflation is running
at a high rate. In such circumstances, if fixed price
tendering is insisted upon, contractors may decline to
tender or else apply prices with such an element of
"cover" for this risk that they become uneconomic. It is
part of the cost consultant's role to advise on this
decision and, if the circumstances are marginal, to seek
tenders on the two alternative bases and to recommend
acceptance according to the results. A good example of
a changing trend in this regard is the United Kingdom
currently, where fixed price tenders have now re-established
themselves as the accepted norm in the wake of the reduced
rate of inflation, after a number of years of high inflation
when fixed price tendering had almost fallen out of use
completely.

32.   If tenders are on a "fluctuations-apply" basis,
there must be satisfactory mechanisms for calculating
them. Traditionally, British contracts allowed for adjustment on the actual basis, involving the auditing of all
movements of individual wage rates and materials and plant
prices. Although accurate, such a method is tedious and
time-consuming and the United Kingdom is now falling in with
the more universal use of indices for price adjustment.

33.   The success of indices is largely a function of
the economic circumstances prevailing at the time of their
application. If the rate of inflation is low or at least
if it is stable, they operate satisfactorily. If rates
of inflation fluctuate widely through the course of a
contract, the indices can generate considerable distortions
on final account amounts. In recent years in the United
Kingdom when the construction market was falling off,

but inflation rates remained high, such was the recovery
by contractors through the index form of adjustment that
it acquired a bad name and cost consultants were recommending a return to the traditional method of audit. In times
of high inflation, fluctuations and the correct prediction
thereof can be the single most important factor in the cost
control process.

34.   A summary of this section is as follows:-

  (i)   While fixed price tenders are desirable,
         there may be circumstances when they are
         not sensible.

  (ii)   This applies particularly to major
         projects and at times of high inflation.

  (iii) There is often advantage in seeking
         tenders on the two alternative bases.

  (iv)   Indices for price adjustment can produce
         distortions compared with market reality.

Final Account 'Claims'

35.   It is an unfortunate fact that the propogation
of final account 'claims' by contractors has become
one of the great growth activities in the construction
industry universally.   This is a function of the volatile
and generally depressed market of the past decade, leading
to keen tendering and the consequent need for contractors
to maximise recovery on any contract change.

36.   The preparation of claims and the settlement
thereof are very large subjects in their own right but
from the viewpoint of cost control, there are a number of
important things to say.

37.   Firstly, it is not always sensible to tie a
contractor down so tightly in the terms of his contract,
that he cannot be fairly recompensed for changed
conditions.   The same can equally apply to extension of
time clauses in the case of which deletions can be so all-
consuming that they leave no capacity for the client or
design team to recognise adverse circumstances.   There is
benefit in drafting documents to allow at least some
loophole for sympathetic treatment.   The danger if this
is not recognised is a permanent situation of confrontation
and much non-productive time and energy spent combating it.

38.   Secondly and to return to an earlier theme, if
claim situations are building up, the cost controller must
recognise these.   By no manner of means does this mean
that he accepts their rectitude, but if he is to do his
job properly, he is obliged to play a double role.   He
will presumably be seeking to counter or minimise on his
client's behalf all claims presented, but he would be
failing in his duty to his client if he did not recognise

their existence in his cost reporting. It is true that
many clients do not appreciate this and see it as some sort
of admission of weakness on the cost consultant's part.
This must be countered for it is the cost controller's
duty to prepare his client for a reasoned and
supportable figure for the settlement of the final account.
If he has done this, he will have carried out his role
successfully and will have done all that he can to avoid
that signal mark of failure of the cost control process,
namely recourse to litigation or arbitration. The mark
of this failure is the likelihood that the client will
spend the substantial costs and time always generated by
such proceedings in arriving at a settlement which
efficient cost control may have suggested originally.

39.   Conclusions of this section are:-

   (i)   It is not always of advantage to impose
         very restricted contract conditions,
         for these lead to situations of
         continuing confrontation.

   (ii) Likelihood and possible cost effect
         of claims must be recognised in the
         cost control procedure.

   (iii) Efficient cost control and early
         warning of final account figures
         minimise the likelihood of resorting
         to litigation.

Discussion on Papers 1–4

MR A.W. HOWITT, formerly of Peat, Marwick, Mitchell Company
I would first like to support a remark in Lord Selsdon's Opening Address. I entirely agree that there is a substantial market for project management in the Middle East. My former firm – and I know the same applies to a number of my former competitors in the audience – has carried out a large amount of management work in Saudi Arabia and elsewhere, albeit more by way of management organisation than by management of projects. We must press on in this field. It has long been my wish – with all respect to other members of the audience – to be involved in the setting up of a building project management organisation which could take on the Bechtels of this world.

In introducing his Paper, Mr Minch referred to a recent decision of the International Finance Corporation (IFC) to encourage less public sector financing and more private sector investment. One is tempted to wonder whether this was really recognising and accepting that the IBRD/IFC were not going to have sufficient funds available in the future.

Mr Minch also referred to the increasing trend towards co-financing. Can he tell the audience how the leader of the finance providers is selected on any project; and how the consultant/contractor can tell who it is, thus avoiding waste of time and money by approaching the wrong party.

I should like to comment on two matters not mentioned in Mr Minch's Paper, but related to it.

The Chancellor's Autumn Statement of 1984 requires a cut in the Foreign and Commonwealth Office (FCO) expenditure, leaving it to the FCO to decide how the cut should be applied as between salaries, expenses, etc., and Aid. It is a fair bet that some of it will fall on Aid, which has been running at around £1 billion a year. Of that sum, the percentage being given through Multilateral Agencies has been steadily rising and by a considerable amount. When representations to the Government are made by the British Consultants' Bureau (BCB) and others that the bilateral aid should not be allowed to drop – not because we fear foreign competition, but because we believe that bilateral aid is much more effective for the UK, in political terms – we are told that, irrespective of whether

Management of international construction projects. Thomas Telford Ltd, London, 1984.

35

we are right or not, the Government has made future
commitments to the Multilateral Agencies and such commitments
cannot be cut. It seems to follow, therefore, that any cut in
Aid next year will fall on the bilateral part and that the cut
will be substantial. This should be resisted at all costs.

With regard to the Export Credits Guarantee Department
(ECGD), I am not yet convinced of the sins of error or
omission of this Department. Over the years, I have heard
numerous complaints that it was too difficult to obtain cover
from ECGD; I have never heard one complaint or suggestion that
cover was being given too easily. There is an inherent and
inevitable conflict between the requirements of ECGD to break
even and the desire of every consultant and contractor to
obtain cover on every contract, no matter how risky the latter
may be.

Turning now to some detailed points in Mr Minch's very
interesting Paper. The Table on page 1 is relevant to the
first point I made; it shows the rise of the MDB disbursements
and the fall in official development assistance and export
credits. Are the 1983 figures available and has Mr Minch any
estimates for 1984?

On page 2, paragraph 1, could it be argued that the
situation to which reference is made - the developing
countries receiving less in new loans than they had to spend
servicing old ones - had been artificially avoided in previous
years as a result of excessive and imprudent commercial
lending, rather than being brought about in 1983 by any
undesirable curtailment of such lending?

For the reasons stated, I agree with the second paragraph on
page 2 that the influence of MDB disbursements is much greater
than the arithmetic figure of 12 percent indicates.

With reference to the Table on page 2, I am surprised that
out of a total of 14.5 billion US dollars, Water and Sewerage
account for only 0.8 billion US dollars. I would have thought
that they would and should account for more. I am not sure
how agricultural irrigation projects are dealt with in the
figures.

Mr Minch has set out in some detail the stages -
identification, appraisal, and so on - through which a project
has to pass. I suspect that most of us would agree that the
bank staff play their parts efficiently and courteously in
this process. One suspects, however, that periodically the
rules are bent to allow loans to be given for politically
desirable projects in politically acceptable countries.
Moreover, corruption practised by officials in borrowing
countries - virtually unheard of in connection with bank
projects 15 or 20 years ago - does now seem to be reluctantly
accepted by bank staff, particularly in certain countries
which I will not name.

With regard to co-financing, I would like more information
on who leads and how one would know who leads.

On page 5, paragraph 2, there is a reference to new
financial instruments having been introduced by the Bank in

1983. It would be helpful to have more details about this.

At the bottom of page 6 and top of page 7, Mr Minch compares the criteria for an IFC investment with those for a bank loan. I am tempted to wonder whether they should not be the same. Why should new bank loans 'originate as the perception of a market opportunity', and should banks not provide proper answers to the questions listed at the foot of page 7 and top of page 8? Why, indeed, at the top of page 9, does the procedure differ for plant and equipment supply?

Finally, when I was in Abu Dhabi three weeks ago, I was told by an executive of one of the Funds that British quoted prices were competitive, but that the British were much more inclined than others to operate the 'fine print' of these quotations and thereby to claim extras. Does Mr Minch have any comments on this?

MR R.J. BRIDLE, Mitchell Cotts Ltd

This contribution is made from the point of view of a former Public Sector Client. The public sector, too, has to assess risk and it uses the conditions of contract to allocate it.

With reference to Paper 3, while Mr South is right that insurance is important, it is not the only, or necessarily the most important, subject in analysis and allocation. In general, client governments carry their own insurance against real risks, like failure, in distinction from risks such as the contractor may face if, at the time of tender, he fails properly to understand the allocation. This is because bearing the consequences of adverse events cannot be compensated by an internal transfer payment, nor will insurance, if paid from external sources, fully cover the many economic knock-ons.

The government client will, therefore, pass on risk wherever it is in his interests to do so to promote efficiency. However, many risks can be avoided during preparation, but often insufficient thought is given to doing so. Economic analysis is possible through a hypothetical insurance model derived from multiplying risk by the economic consequence and handling uncertainty explicitly. It is not necessary to discuss the mathematics here; it is sufficient to say that the client will find it worthwhile to put preparation effort into reducing risk and/or economic consequences until the input equals the reduction in notional insurance. It follows that only those risks which are interdependent with those of the contractor, and which the contractor can reduce by skill, or at least price rationally, or will affect his behaviour for the better, should be passed on. However, while such an approach is logical, behaviour is unlikely to be so dispassionate; or as Mr South observes, 'the most important single factor is the inbuilt prejudices and risk attitudes of the parties involved'.

Many countries learn from us but, unfortunately, they do not always sift what they learn. The principles of the ICE Conditions of Contract have remained consistent through time,

37

Table 1

Engineering	Financial	Political
Unknown ground	Prices/costs inflation	Impositions by governments
Uncertain quality and quantity of natural materials	Exchange rates	Import controls
Untried method of execution	Interest rates	Exchange controls
Uncertain reliability of construction equipment	Wages, rates, drop in productivity, strikes	Changing employment laws
Quality/delivery man-made goods	Delayed payment, bad debts	Arbitrary denial of legal redress
Weather/natural disaster	Delays against construction schedules	Riot, revolution, war
Design error		

but the administration of contracts has changed. The professional manpower committed by both the client and the contractor in this country has escalated, and that behaviour has been exported. Such behaviour as Mr South observes is adversarial, concerned to contest the allocation and assessment of risk during the course of the contract.

The financial and political risks are additional to the engineering risks and are set out in Table 1. In general, civil administration, on account of risk-adverse attitudes, is likely to pass on more of these risks than is economically justifiable, and often there is contention during the course of the contract, despite explicit spelling out of responsibilities.

It is, therefore, very sensible for anyone concerned with assessing risk in other countries to take account of HMG's assessment through ECGD, who rank countries in a number of categories. However, that ranking seems to be close to following GNP per capita and it is reasonable to suppose that financial and political risks are greater in those countries where GNP per capita is smaller. Instability is most likely where people are poorest, and GNP/head expresses, to a degree, the state of the people. It is unlikely to be the only variable and discussion may suggest other indicators. However, given some exceptions, the indicator may be reasonable.

Where a project represents a substantial proportion of a country's wealth, and risks are likely to be priced according to the perception described, it will be more economic for that country to spread general risks over the whole economy. It will also attract more bids and investment. As a country grows wealthier, the need to spread the risk applies only to increasingly longer contracts. Contract strategies will be related to the five categories of GNP per capita, namely under £170; £170-£330; £330-£1,560; £1,560-3,650; and over £3,650. Projects will best be administered under different forms of contract between direct labour at one end and a lump sum contract with heavy liquidated damages at the other. The middle ground of this spectrum is therefore of considerable interest in respect of the optimum allocation of risk.

In the late 1970s, the EDC for Civil Engineering took an interest in the target cost form of contract, particularly in its risk sharing and participative aspects. The EDC were interested in two aspects: how the form of contract could reduce adversarial behaviour; and how the allocation risks could be optimally shared. The EDC argued that the client would be better off if he undertook more risk himself, sharing it over many schemes. It was also thought that there was an appropriate level of contract size above which the contract should fall in the middle ground of contract form. That categorisation is shown in Table 2. There are upper levels and the behaviour induced by target cost may make its adoption appropriate at lower levels.

Table 2

Category	GNP/Capita	Size of contract for middle ground
1	< £340	£1m
2	£340–660	£3m
3	£660–3120	£10m
4	£3120–7300	£30m
5	> £7300	£100m

There are, of course, other forms of contract apart from the target cost in the middle ground.

To conclude, the propositions put forward in this contribution are that, first, large public sector clients should think much harder about the form of contract adopted, and the behaviour it induces through the way in which the contract shares risk; and second, they should think much harder about their own behaviour in administering contracts and the real cost of that administration.

DR MARTIN BARNES, Martin Barnes and Partners

With reference to Paper 3, I would first like to make an observation about the Paper and then ask Mr South a question. The observation is that, in my experience of international projects, there is a need to look at all the risks and uncertainties associated with the work in setting up the management strategy, not just at those which may or may not be insurable. This is an essential precursor to making the insurance arrangements as it involves the larger decisions of how the risks in total and in particular should be allocated as between the employer and contractor.

There is a tendency to think of the risks which have to be allocated only as those which may be insured – these generally are the low probability, high impact risks. Construction projects are also assailed by high probability, low impact risks and those which are of medium probability and medium impact. A policy for allocation of all of them is necessary if the incentives to control and manage the work are to be distributed in the interests of achieving a successful project.

Broadly speaking, risks should be placed with the party involved in the management of the scheme who is best able to manage the factor which gives rise to the risk. This is why, for example, one would normally allocate the risk of plant and labour output varying from expectation upon the contractor. It is his particular skill to both foresee and control these factors. If he cannot foresee and control a particular factor influencing the outcome of the project, such as inflation or changed currency exchange rates, it is sensible to limit his total risk exposure by leaving these risks to be carried by the client. Risks should be subcontracted to insurers only if the cost benefit to the client or contractor justifies doing so. This policy generally leads to insurance of the low probability, high impact risks, but makes questionable insurance of such risks as delay to completion.

This brings me to my question. In his Paper, Mr South suggests that delayed completion of construction might be insurable. I would like him to give more information about this. Is it possible to insure against delays, however caused, or only against delay caused for particular reasons? How does the level of premium charged relate to the liquidated damages which would otherwise be levied against the contractor - presumably it is much lower. Where such insurance has been used, can we be reassured that the dilution of the pressure to complete on time which insuring the risk brings, has not itself led to the occurrence of the event against which the insurance was taken out.

MR SOUTH

The insurance market offers only two solutions to the problem of delay risk. Both have advantages but neither is ideal.

The most usual solution favoured is the adoption of a so-called Advance Profits policy. This basically indemnifies the owner for delay in start-up attributable to claims under the construction insurance. The delay risk can also be extended to cover claims resulting from shipments of key items of equipment under a marine cargo policy. This coverage is not particularly easy to understand, is expensive, and has very little usefulness to a large public works owner whose project has no immediate revenue or discernible profit.

What of the contractor? Delay risks are traditionally passed down to him by means of liquidated damages provisions and there is, or used to be, a market in Lloyd's for this class. It has now virtually disappeared, not I hasten to say because of any failure of nerve by underwriters, but because the results over the years have been disastrous. Underwriters stand very little chance of writing an adequate spread of risks and more often than not tend to get offered only risks of above average severity. Most underwriters, therefore, quite understandably view applications for liquidated damage insurance with considerable scepticism, on the basis that the proposer knows the real odds much better than the underwriter!

One of the main reasons why the insurance world has not come up with an answer to the delay risk is because construction underwriters are not concerned with, nor usually empowered to write, the operating risk. In overseas countries particularly, the operating risk is normally the preserve of the local market, and even if the owner is content to leave the construction insurances to his contractor, he will invariably arrange the operating insurances himself. A project orientated insurance package is what is required. However, if a package deal (consisting of the marine cargo, construction testing and, say, the first two years' operating risks) were to be presented to insurers, it would need a combination of factors, both intricate and difficult to arrange, to bring it off successfully: namely the active cooperation of contractor and owner, total trust and confidence on both sides and insurance procurement of a high order. I appreciate this is probably utopian at the moment, but considering the enormous attention that the construction insurances receive, and the bitter competition they engender, it is surprising that the delay risk, frequently as significant as the construction insurance, is so often ignored and left uninsured.

To answer the specific points which Dr Barnes raises, I do not think that underwriters would ever contemplate insuring against delays, however caused. Although strike insurance schemes have been attempted in the past, the results have invariably been disappointing for the reasons Dr Barnes has observed, namely that the existence of strike insurance is a disincentive for the insured to settle with his labour force. As regards the level of premium, I do not think it realistic to compare it to the premiums for liquidated damages. There always is, or was, an element of 'penalty rate' about this class and, quite frankly, a good deal of speculative and entrepreneurial underwriting. Project delay premium rates might be half as much again as the CAR/EAR rates, but the substantial underpinning of a project's bankability that the existence of such a policy would provide, would make such a policy extremely cost-effective.

DR MARTIN BARNES, Martin Barnes and Partners

In paragraph 9 of Paper 4, Mr Coates claims that the priced bill of quantities used in the United Kingdom produces a most valuable by-product in that it provides data with which cost control throughout the design stage can be achieved. Although I am an enthusiast for using bills of quantities for contractors' estimating and for subsequent valuation of variations, I have never found that prices from other bills of quantities are much help during design.

The decisions which have most impact upon the final cost of the project are those taken in the early stages of design. Characteristically, this is before quantities of work can be established at a level of detail of a conventional bill of quantities. In any case, for international projects, and particularly for engineering projects rather than building projects, the relevance of prices derived from another completed project to decision making on the current project is quite small. The current project is likely to be in a different part of the world, to contain quite different permanent work and to be carried out in significantly different commercial conditions. If forcing cost control upon designers is left until the design has reached a stage where bill of quantities pricing can be simulated, it may be too late. Designers faced with forecast cost over-runs will claim that things have gone too far to be changed, that somebody else must find savings in another part of the project or, as a last resort, that the client must find the extra money because his project will be deficient if he does not.

This approach to cost control does not lead to real control. It is desperately important to establish real control over decision making by designers right at the beginning of the design process. This means forcing them to consider the cost implications of all the decisions they make.

I have found that the best approach is to use a 'top down' approach to cost control. This comprises setting sectional budgets for the parcels of work which are the responsibility of particular designers or of specialist groups within the design team. The budgets made available to them at the beginning of design are those which, when added together and when a substantial contingency allowance is added, produce the figure which was the client's expectation of the total cost as embodied in the feasibility study. The overall project manager must disburse these very large contingency allowances to section managers only a little at a time, with the greatest reluctance, and after the latter have fought their case for more money with considerable energy and supporting evidence. This process may seem crude, but it has the major advantages of forcing concentration upon cost into the minds of designers right at the beginning of the design process and of forcing early and vigorous reconsideration of the balance of expected cost between sectors of the project. Any alternative arrangement which has a taint of postponing the cost check until better data are available almost inevitably leads to leaving the cost check until too late.

My second observation on Mr Coates's Paper is to register disagreement with his conclusion that cost control gets more difficult the further the work progresses through the construction stage of a project. My experience is exactly the reverse. The approach which we use in managing projects, international or otherwise, is to direct attention in the name of cost control at the decisions made affecting the remaining work. Nothing about the work already done can still be controlled and it is only the remaining work which is susceptible to control in any real sense. It is most difficult to exert control in the early stages when most work has yet to be done and least is known about what it is, when,

by whom and how it is going to be done. When construction is
under way the remaining work is well defined, the options for
how it is to be carried out are well constrained, and the
knowledge of the cost impact of those decisions which remain
to be taken is better than at any earlier stage. These
factors make control easier in the later stages than in the
earlier stages.

5 Turnkey projects

F. R. DONOVAN, John Brown Engineers and
Constructors Ltd, London

1. INTRODUCTION

2. THE LEARNING CURVE

3. NEGOTIATIONS

4. FINANCE & PAYMENT

5. LANGUAGE PROBLEMS

6. GETTING GOING

7. TEAM LEADERS

8. MEETING THE CLIENT

9. COMMUNICATIONS

10. CLIENT INSPECTORATE

11. ESTABLISHMENT & ACCOMMODATION

12. PERSONNEL MATTERS

13. CLEARING CUSTOMS

14. TRANSPORTATION & HANDLING OF MATERIALS

15. INSURANCE

16. USING LOCAL LABOUR

17. PLANNING PROGRESS & COST CONTROL

18. PRE-ASSEMBLED UNITS

19. ENGINEERING & CONSTRUCTION CO-OPERATION

20. INSPECTION STANDARDS

21. CONSTRUCTION & PRE-COMMISSIONING

22. ACCEPTANCE CERTIFICATES

23. CONCLUSIONS

INTRODUCTION

1. It is difficult to say anything new about Turnkey
Projects. The subject has already received much attention from
experienced contractors. Some aspects of Turnkey Projects are
the subject matter of other papers being given during this
Conference, Risk Analysis, Cost Control, Finance to mention a
few. It was, therefore, decided to discuss an actual Project
and mention a number of aspects from this Turnkey Project which
occurred, how these were or might have been overcome and to
suggest points which should be carefully considered at tender
stage of a future contract and how these might be solved. The
list of points that could be considered is long and it is hoped
that those that have been chosen will prove interesting.

THE LEARNING CURVE

1. Shortly after the end of the French/Algerian war in 1962
Sonatrach, the Algerian National Oil Company (Sonatrach is an
acronym for 'Societe Nationale de Transportation et Commercial-
isation des Hydrocarbures') came out to tender on the international market for a 24" crude oil line from Hassi Messaoud to
Arzew, a distance of some 800 kilometres. John Brown Engineers
& Constructors Limited (JBE&C), formerly known as Constructors
John Brown Limited (CJB), who were at that time seeking to
extend their known pipe-laying capabilities, tendered for the
contract, and despite severe international opposition, were
awarded the contract. Thus began a period of activity in
Algeria.

2. It is not my intention to discuss this particular
contract, its history is very well known. CJB made a film of
the construction phase of this contract which has been shown
many times in many countries.

3. The contract was well designed, the procurement successfully achieved and the pipe-laying carried out at the required
rate. Financially the project was a disaster. However, over
the 24 months activity we learned a great deal, thus it was
decided to capitalise on this knowledge and continue to work in
Algeria.

NEGOTIATIONS

1. There followed a number of conceptual design studies for
Sonatrach, followed by two more detailed studies for a further
16" unstabilised line from Hassi Messaoud to Arzew and an LPG
Plant at Arzew to receive, stabilise the condensate and liquify
the gas to Propane and Butane. The process plant was put out
to tender and with some assistance perhaps from Sonatrach, but
only after nine months of difficult negotiation, CJB were
awarded a Turnkey Contract for detailed design, procurement,
construction, pre-commissioning and assistance in operation.
Thus, in December 1970 work began in London.

2. It will be remembered that it was only in 1962 that the
French/Algerian war came to a conclusion with the withdrawal of
the French. Whilst by 1970 conditions were normal and calm,

NEGOTIATIONS (CONTINUED)

2. (Cont'd) the thing most noticeable to Western Europeans visiting Algeria was the youth of Algerian Managers one met. All these young managers were very helpful and eager to assist in their country's development but despite their titles they lacked both the experience and responsibility to make decisions, which led to many problems.

3. Due to their limited experience with Turnkey Projects, Sonatrach appointed another Company to act as a Management Contractor, incorporating within their terms of reference the responsibility to review all design matters, and inspect all phases of material fabrication, both in Vendors Works on Site. This Company is later referred to as the "Inspectorate".

4. The negotiations centred around a fixed lump sum, much time was spent on ensuring that the scope of work was well defined, such that no extras could be granted, other than by addition by Sonatrach. Thus, we had the worst of all worlds, total responsibility and no possibility of increase to the agreed price.

FINANCE & PAYMENT

1. All aspects of contract discussions are important, but financial conditions of overseas Turnkey Projects are even more so. During any Turnkey Project outside influences may change, for example, change of government, change of policy. Such possibilities must be considered and the qualifying clauses deemed necessary by the Contractor negotiated. The extent of exchange control facilities should be understood to avoid the possibility of monies being locked up at the end of the Contract.

2. During the term of our Contract duration, and to-date, the Dinar was not convertible on the World Currency Market.

3. The form of payment and the guarantee of receipt of such payment is paramount. Various bodies exist to provide an insurance against non-payment. Certain countries are greater risks than others as will be seen by the size of premium being charged by E.C.G.D. Some countries are blacklisted due to their poor risk levels and even the alternative Irrevocable Letter of Credit needs, in some instances, to be carefully scrutinised, especially in the case of a fringe banking organisation. One must beware delays in receiving interim valuation or down-payments, especially in the early period of a contract whilst the bureaucratic process is being established. Finance costs can be high and drastically effect the cash flow situation.

LANGUAGE PROBLEMS

1. The common language in Algeria is Arabic but French is spoken by all reasonably educated Algerians. Technical or commercial Algerians who have been further educated abroad will probably speak an additional language. The Contract language was French and all our discussions were therefore carried out in French with frequent asides by the Algerians in Arabic.

LANGUAGE PROBLEMS (CONTINUED)

1. (Cont'd) We found it unwise to attempt to negotiate in French. Once discussions became serious all comments were made to the Algerians through an interpreter. This sounds simple but one must find someone who has a comprehensive knowledge of the two tongues, understands the niceties of contracting and does not become emotionally involved with the argument. After much trial and error we found it better to employ a bi-lingual female, born or blessed with a preference to the English language. It is so important that the interpreter accurately understands ones point of view. This meant that meetings took longer and despite care to avoid misunderstandings, misunderstandings did occur. Even when all points have been discussed and apparent understanding achieved, when one receives the written confirmation, in French, translation shows that differences have crept in. This is a problem that one has to accept. The difficulty to find good translators is equally daunting. Few people are really bi-lingual in all respects. Perfect speaking Frenchmen or Frenchwomen, translating English tend to be mesmerised by the English text and the French version comes out slightly stilted and somewhat Franglais. In truth, the Algerians often told us that they found our French slightly odd and I presume they were being polite.

GETTING GOING

1. To undertake any Turnkey Project is daunting. To undertake a Turnkey Project in the United Kingdom requires experience and determination. To undertake a fixed price Turnkey Project overseas, particularly in a country trying very hard to establish its newly won self-determination, requires the above attributes plus all the luck going.

2. We had been responsible for the preparation of the Appel d'Offre (Call for Tenders). We thus appreciated the detailed engineering outstanding. Furthermore, we had already made contact with suppliers, thus completing the engineering and ordering materials was straightforward and was proceeded with energetically. The Inspectorate at this stage agreed our specifications and certified sub-contractors welders. In most technologies they were routinely efficient and caused no delay to the completion of the design.

3. It will be remembered that in 1970 the rate of inflation was low, suppliers were prepared to make competitive offers and accept demanding requirements, and were able to offer and maintain acceptable deliveries. Thus, the U.K. involvement proceeded well.

4. Our problems began as we moved ourselves and our equipment into Algeria.

TEAM LEADERS

1. It is profitable to dwell on the choice of the Project Manager and the Resident Manager. For obvious reasons, the most important being that he must control both the London and Site end, we decided that the Project Manager should share his

TEAM LEADERS (CONTINUED)

1. (Cont'd) time between both localities. Whilst this was demanding, it ensured an overall awareness of everything. It was further decided that he should be the main contact with the Client on all financial and contractual matters. All correspondence from Sonatrach or the Inspectorate was referred to the P.M. and all replies originated from London. The volume of correspondence was heavy but the technical facilities, the translation and typing facilities were all more easily available in London. This allowed the R.M. to concentrate on the construction of the L.P.G. Plant.

2. The Resident Engineer was a Scotsman, experienced in fixed lump sum construction contracts. Despite an autocratic attitude and a disciplinarian, he was nevertheless respected by his own staff and by the Algerians and in due course by the "Engineer". The term "Engineer" here is used exactly as defined in the ICE Conditions of Contract. Though unable to speak French, by some odd quirk his precise and basic instructions in English were apparently clearly understood by the locals.

MEETING THE CLIENT

1. This division of responsibilities proved effective and allowed each to concentrate on his strengths. Of note, is the requirement in developing countries for frequent meetings with the Client. It is normal for these meetings to be used as training grounds for Client staff. It is the practice for these employees to sit in a row behind their masters, assiduously taking verbatim notes. One wonders just what was made of the numerous versions submitted to their superiors each day. Few of the meetings were constructive in the sense that decisions were made or answers given to questions. Certainly, as elements of the plant reached completion, the number of Algerian employees walking round the site watching the work proceeding reached disconcerting numbers and there were sometimes two or three groups at the same time.

COMMUNICATIONS

1. Communication with Head Office is essential. Such communication must be in a form that is unambiguous, allows distribution and later reference. Writing letters from overseas and using available postal facilities can mean serious delays. Telephone calls often involve long delays and the quality of speech may be poor. We made a decision that all communication would be by telex. In Europe and Northern Africa the telex service is good and delays are minimal. Writing a telex imposes a thinking discipline, whereas telephoning encourages discussion. Weather conditions are of no consequence if one requires prompt information or advice. A permanent record is, therefore, available and has proved an absolute necessity to prompt failing memories, moreover the receipt of a telex tends to speed up the response. Telephone calls should be limited only to the most urgent reasons.

49

COMMUNICATIONS (CONTINUED)

2. We insisted that every traveller acted as a courier, handcarrying items to and from Site. The surcharges at the outgoing airport are small compared with the possible cost at Site due to the absence of small but important items.

3. Local Customs officials, certainly in Algeria, at that time, were reasonable and allowed suitcases through customs, provided a suitable "Cover Note" was signed. This allowed the Site to clear the paperwork next day.

4. The moral is that once involved in an overseas Turnkey Project, everyone must participate.

CLIENT INSPECTORATE

1. Another difficulty imposed by the "Engineer" was his appointment of an Inspectorate, a well known French Company. Though punctilious in their professional behaviour and despite private thoughts about Algeria, they acted very correctly but paying great attention to detail, interpreting drawings and specifications to a degree that stretched our patience to its limits. The Inspectorate were responsible for agreeing our monthly valuations and here their unwillingness to certify led to considerable acrimonious argument.

ESTABLISHMENT & ACCOMMODATION

1. The first concern of our Resident Manager at Arzew was how to house CJB's staff employees. The work load indicated that a field team of 500 hands would be required, 100 JBE&C and 400 Algerians. How to house 100 ex-pats? The options were to build a camp, import pre-assembled cabins or find local accommodation. After consideration it was decided to find local accommodation. There was, in 1969/70, a certain amount of private enterprise in existence, a local property owner was located, who agreed an acceptable lease on reasonable terms for a large appartment. The appartment was rebuilt to contain 50 cabin-type rooms, each adequate for two men. Much though was given whether to provide single or double rooms. It was decided that shared rooms were preferable to ensure that minimum brooding or introspection during the long evenings, particularly since we had decided to give contracts to CJB staff on a single stay 18 months contract. Laundry facilities were laid on, staffed by local Algerians but no food was provided. Arrangements were soon made with local cafes for meals. The rebuilding of the appartments was expensive but proved to be a good decision, it kept the men together, it gave them privacy from each other and from the local population and whilst some drinking went on in quarters, any excessive bouts were contained in-house and were a minimum bother to the locals. The accommodation was fortunately only 1 km from site.

2. At the time of our Contract, accommodation in all forms was lacking, Sonatrach had no Company accommodation available and we had to meet the needs and economics of our Contract as cheaply as possible. It was, therefore, not possible to build camps or bring in pre-fabricated buildings though subsequently

Sonatrach policies changed and Contractors were requested to set up site camps.

PERSONNEL MATTERS

1. The weather in Western Algeria, particularly around Arzew, is mild in winter and acceptably hot in summer. A westerly wind blows and one is spared the humidity experienced in Algiers. There is some rain in late winter and early spring April produces heavy storms but most winter days have some sun. For most of their days on site the men stripped to the waist and all developed quite striking suntans. This quite pleasant climate certainly helped to solve many working and personal problems.

2. Whenever the men decided to have an evening in Oran, some 60 kilometres away, special arrangements were made, buses could be hired or the R.E. would allocate site transport. Whilst Oran is certainly bigger, it provided few pleasures that could not be found in Arzew, thus the number of visits were minimal, most went when they went, merely for a change of environment.

3. Concessions were made to a few senior members of the staff, the R.E., his three Senior Construction Engineers and the Administrator. These five were given a car and accommodation some two kilometres from Arzew with married status. This number was rigidly adhered to and became accepted by the CJB team. The eighteen month contract precluded any return trips to the U.K., leave was taken in Algeria, many arranged for wives and family to come to Oran or Algiers on holiday. The subsistence terms arranged allowed this without detracting too much from the financial gain all hoped to achieve by overseas employment.

4. Certain parts of the world hold dangers to health and human wellbeing. The standards available and those required for medical facilities must be ascertained in advance. It may be necessary to provide a Doctor for the project and to be well prepared for emergencies which might require air transportation to another country. In areas of malaria or cholera proper monitoring facilities must be arranged to ensure correct medication.

5. A situation occurred in Arzew where a staff employee had a car accident necessitating immediate transfer to a hospital in France. This entailed making arrangements to hire a light plane to fly to Marseilles. We were fortunate that all this proved possible but we reflected what might have happened in less civilised areas.

6. Religion or local customs may well affect a project – a different working week from that in the U.K., additional statutory holidays, acceptance or non-acceptance of other religious sects on the same work-site, admission of female staff, secretarial or nursing and any hostility that may exist towards ex-patriate supervision. There are certain jobs which may be taboo in some circumstances. All these aspects must be examined and understood before making contractual commitments.

CLEARING CUSTOMS

1. I suppose that the U.K.'s customs clearance procedures for foreign imports would appear to a first time importer from Algeria complicated and bureaucratic, endless forms, dues to pay, and so on. The Algerian system, despite our experience, still seemed complicated, we clearly could not handle the paperwork ourselves, a reputable and knowledgeable agent was required.

2. We made overtures to the appropriate State controlled Department. It had only just been formed, their employees were, if anything, more innocent than ourselves. We remembered only too well our problems to import and subsequently export construction plant equipment on our previous construction contract.

3. Fortunately we were given some direction by our Client, who wanted his plant built to programme. He introduced us to an agent acquainted with all aspects of customs procedures who, over the whole of our project programme, protected us from ourselves and officialdom. That this service cost a certain amount of money cannot be denied, but the benefit to us was inestimable.

TRANSPORTATION & HANDLING OF MATERIALS

1. It will be useful to mention the difficulties met in shipping materials to Algeria. Regular ships are available from U.K. ports to Oran and Algiers. Adequate packing is essential if materials are to arrive on site undamaged and whilst U.K. stevedores are not famed for their gentleness, their efforts compare favourably with scenes witnessed at foreign ports. One of the principal tools used by the mediterranean stevedore is the fork-lift truck. Pipes or fittings, carefully handled off the boat, laid on the quayside are attacked by a fork-lift driver. Regardless of exhortations, he lowers his fork and charges and scoops up materials, raises the fork and charges a waiting lorry, depositing the whole with noise and sparks into the lorry. Bevelled ends of pipes protected by plastic caps are now exposed to the inevitable consequences as other materials are loaded. Warning cries are ignored and with a smile on completion one is assured that all is "Tres bien fait". What can one do.

2. Very little, that is how things are done and one puts things right on the site. It costs time and effort but one is pleased to get the materials into the proper hands to keep the construction programme going.

3. This is not to say that transportation by sea is without worry. One specifies one's preference to deck or hold but some items must go as deck cargo. To get to Algeria cargo boats pass through the Bay of Biscay where severe storms are frequent. We lost materials at sea, a much needed stack, fabricated, painted and packed, complete with guys, bolts and nuts, etc., was washed overboard in the Bay of Biscay. Yet it is quite remarkable how quickly one can replace such an item. All the drawings and specifications are available, the procedures are

TRANSPORTATION & HANDLING OF MATERIALS (CONTINUED)

3. (Cont'd) known, the fabricator knows just what to do and the time can be cut by 50%.

4. Certain countries hold "black lists" of goods which may not be acceptable in their projects due to their suppliers being 'enemy' nationalities. This can be particularly relevant for example in certain Moslem countries.

INSURANCE

1. Damage to materials involves insurance where making econ-omies is a risky business. In this field, advice should be taken. JBE&C has a subsidiary company specialising in insur-ance. We thus avoided the pitfalls without being persuaded into unnecessary cover. There does exist, of course, mandatory Algerian insurance regulations with respect to site construc-tion which must be adhered to. I do not believe we ever made a successful claim on the Algerian insurances, though we cer-tainly paid the premiums. It is important that all incidents be carefully and accurately noted, records and costs of the consequences filed so that the claim when submitted contains all the facts. It is useless trying to re-construct a case after the events. Witnesses must be contacted at the time and affidavits signed. Many cases are rejected because of this neglect. The important thing to remember is that Insurance Companies are in the business to take premiums, not to pay out claims.

2. One must ensure that Plant insurance is sufficient to allow for local conditions, for example, a machine written off may require import duty paid upon it if it was only in the country on a temporary importation agreement. Spares are sub-ject to different import and customs regulations than those applying to whole machines if damaged parts need to be replaced.

USING LOCAL LABOUR

1. It is of importance when constructing units overseas to use local labour, subject to cost and skills available. Having made a decision during the estimate stage to work to a basis of one ex-patriat to four local workmen, once established, a recruiting drive commenced. In 1970 there was little construc-tion going on at Arzew and thus the response was good. We established a small compound complete with office and drew up a register of all the men and their skills who came to see us. Unfortunately, few skills applicable to a petro-chemical plant were offered. It was therefore decided to train local men, each to a single skill. Many of the men coming from an agri-cultural background, unemployed due to rapid farm mechanisation had never used modern mechanical tools. Thus, we had to teach them to saw, hammer, tighten nuts, things quite fundamental. Fortunately, the locals showed aptitude to such skills and rapidly achieved a level that allowed us to use them on the site. However, we only found two or three local welders whom we were able to train to a standard acceptable to the Inspectorate.

USING LOCAL LABOUR (CONTINUED)

2. Though not fast workers, the local men worked steadily at an acceptable pace and overall gave value for money. They showed themselves adaptable and as one trade tailed off and labour became available we taught them another task and thus gave continuity of employment. We found the Algerians cheerful in character, patient and willing and had few problems during our stay.

3. Using local sub-contractors was also a revealing experience. We were encouraged by Sonatrach to use locals and thus spend local currency. Having established a contract, such as Painting, where the sub-contractor had "permanent" staff, the sub-contractor would arrive on site, complete with accommodation, i.e. tents, make camp and live on the site until the job was done. The advantages were demonstrable and with favourable weather this and similar trades gave few problems.

4. Surprisingly, bricklaying also gave no trouble. One does not expect such skills in a country where concrete is favoured since bricks are imported. We had difficulty agreeing an acceptable method of fireproofing columns and vessels, but finally agreed with the Inspectorate to use a quality firebrick. These we imported from France. The Algerians, after some tuition, showed themselves adept bricklayers and produced a neat economic job.

5. There are, of course, many local taxes which must be paid, for most of which there are today comparable UK taxes. These must be very carefully investigated at pre-tender stage to avoid any omissions, as there are a number of hidden emoluments that will eventually have to be paid.

6. We let the Insulation sub-contract to a West German company, adopting injected polyurethene. They started off with ex-patriat labour, but realising the potential of the locals, reduced their ex-patriat staff to the minimum and employed locals elsewhere, producing an acceptable job.

PLANNING, PROGRESS & COST CONTROL

1. Planning, progress and cost control are subjects deserving high priority, particularly when operating a fixed lump sum overseas Turnkey Contract.

2. It is easy to over-elaborate planning, particularly in these days of PERT systems, coupled to a computer. Such systems do not generate themselves but require effort to ascertain movement, check and feed in information which costs money. How far does one go and to what degree should a site depend on its Head Office for updates. In the early 1970's mini-computers were only just beginning to appear, microcomputers were not then considered. It was very much a situation where one resolved ones problems on site. A C.P.N. was agreed at Head Office with a full Construction input. Activities were limited to about 1,500 and the Site Planner was charged to monitor events and prepare his own mini-activity networks for particular site areas. Every six months, based on information from the Site Planner, Head Office examined the

PLANNING, PROGRESS & COST CONTROL (CONTINUED)

2. (Cont'd) outstanding activities, amended the C.P.N., re-assessed the resource situation and produced an updated printout with a detailed analysis. This was transmitted to Site who considered the situation in the light of this information and made changes, where necessary or possible. This worked well and limited costs. Possibly on larger jobs a more sophisticated approach might be necessary but one must beware of over-indulgence in sorts and schedules. Resident Manager's concentration seems to be in inverse proportion to the Planners enthusiasm and computer printouts.

3. There are so many hick-ups that occur on overseas projects that it is extremely difficult to maintain a modern, sophisticated computerised system up to date.

4. Equally important is measurement of progress on site. Methods vary from full measurement of everything by Quantity Surveyors to casual judgements by the Site Administrator with an assessment of manhours expended to date compared with budget manhours. Some sites take progress of pipework as an overall indicator, pipework using a high percentage of manhours, but this and similar methods tend to be very optimistic and are subject to severe correction at about 60% completion. JBE&C have always had a practical progress system where all activities have an appropriate manhour loading. Activities are readily identified and progress assessed against manhour expenditure. Where progress does not conform to the manhour estimate, additional manhours must be added to the forecast to completion to avoid self-deception. Progress must be identified independently of manhours spent.

5. Cost control requirements are split between Head Office and Site, engineering, materials and management being controlled from Head Office. Skillful purchasing will effect savings and is an area where hard bargaining must be undertaken. Engineering costs are always of concern and must be vigorously controlled, overtime must be an exception and all timesheets rigorously checked weekly. The state of Company's engineering loading is relevant. If the engineering workload is at all slack, misbookings will occur.

6. It is on site where real cost savings can be made. The overall level of understanding by design engineers of their relationship with construction has, I believe, lessened over the last decade. Sites are presented with drawings which do not optimise construction experience. Site engineers must examine all construction details with a critical eye and call for adjustments when considered necessary. These demands must not affect design integrity. Mechanical or hand application, pre-fabrication off-site, pre-fabrication or pre-assembly, all must be considered and the most apposite accepted.

7. The results of progress made are further handled by the cost controllers. Costs are compared with budgets and trend charts produced to highlight differences. These records are vital because if the R.M. is transferred, completion reported as 95% and all difficult elements completed, if a lesser indi-

PLANNING, PROGRESS & COST CONTROL (CONTINUED)

7. (Cont'd) vidual is left to complete and overspends by 10%, who is to blame? An examination of the progress and cost control data should enable the facts to be established.

PRE-ASSEMBLED UNITS

1. Since completion of the Algerian L.P.G. Plant, an old concept has been revised and enlarged. The P.A.U. is very much with us. Offshore requirements forced clients and contractors to rethink their philosophies to ensure that major construction works were undertaken onshore, undercover to shop standards. Tonnages have risen until P.A.U.'s of 2,000 tonnes are now acceptable. The Sullom Voe Project used this method extensively, fabricating about a 100 major P.A.U.'s with a maximum weight of 500 tonnes.

2. On overseas Turnkey Projects, P.A.U.'s can provide an answer to cost and progress problems. Where site facilities are lacking such as accommodation and skilled labour, providing suitable landing points are available, providing suitable road access is available to the site. P.A.U.'s may be the answer. Fabrication is done under known conditions, agreed cost and programme. It is unnecessary to dwell on the P.A.U. concept, it has already been reported in many papers. However, on any Turnkey Project, the concept needs constant consideration. We as a Company had already accepted the concept when working in Algeria and despatched pre-fabricated skid-mounted assemblies though at that time their weights did not exceed 50 tonnes.

ENGINEERING & CONSTRUCTION CO-OPERATION

1. The relationship between Engineering and Construction is not renowned for its total harmony. Engineering must ever keep one simple objective in mind - prepare all necessary documentation, drawings, etc., order, inspect and expedite all required materials to site to meet an agreed construction programme. To ensure that this requirement is met it is now usual to include in the engineering team experienced construction people. This integration ensures that the needs of site are always in focus, that the design recognises any particular construction problems and that documentation reaches site in time and in the correct order. Priorities may vary between Head Office and site but if there must be arbitration, both sides of the argument will be presented.

2. Since site personnel begrudge any praise of their design offices efforts, it is necessary that designers spend time on sites to understand site problems. Whenever possible site personnel should also spend time in the design office. It is a healthy process and will ensure integrated project teams. The site personnel can play a significant role in ensuring that the maximum flow of statistics is fed back to Engineering. No Resident Engineer should leave site without a complete dossier being prepared reporting problems or matters of interest that occurred and how, if necessary, they were resolved.

INSPECTION STANDARDS

1. Quality Assurance and Control are the words in vogue today but quality of manufacture and fabrication was understood and needed when we were at Arzew. Offshore requirements have compelled a greater degree of codification but the principles remain unchanged. The items specified and ordered should arrive on site conforming to the stated requirements. Why is this not always so?

2. The choice of the supplier is the contractor's perogative. He makes his choice after consideration of the variables of price, delivery and personal knowledge of the supplier. The quality of his Inspectorate is a known factor yet despite having all the major cards the game is not always won. Why?

3. Remedial work required after delivery to site will be time consuming and may have catastrophic cost effects. If it requires heavy cranage, handling delays could be long and widespread. Errors do get missed despite every effort. Calculated risks are sometimes taken when it is considered that time is more important than a known defect. Shipping schedules wait for no man, large payments due on arrival of material at site, cash flow requirements all tend to influence management. It is however when the fault has been missed and surfaces during pre-commissioning or even commissioning that the real cost effect comes home.

4. The efficiency or otherwise of international Client representation and Inspection Agencies will vary upon the nationality interface and the reputation and level of qualification of the Inspectorate. This must be investigated by the contractor before submitting proposals for Turnkey Projects.

5. To maintain a high level of acceptability requires dedication and character from the Inspector, particularly when he is pressurised by his own project team. He must maintain continuity throughout the manufacturing process to ensure consistency of standards. The design office must ensure that the standards demanded are compatible with the duties required, neither excessive nor inadequate.

6. Compared with some foreign companies, the design and quality of some products from British manufacturers is seen sometimes at a disadvantage. It is, therefore, of the utmost importance that a high level of inspection is maintained throughout the project including final protection, packaging and crating. Nothing should be left to chance, assurance that all will be done should be ignored and inspection maintained to the bitter end. Good packaging is vital if all the previous efforts are not to be wasted.

CONSTRUCTION & PRE-COMMISSIONING

1. There is often a conflict of interests between construction staff who put pieces together and pre-commissioning staff who worry that parts fit correctly and will work properly when the plant operates. The need to maintain rotating equipment, particularly when construction personnel are humping materials all around can be extremely vexing to pre-commissioning

CONSTRUCTION & PRE-COMMISSIONING (CONTINUED)

1. (Cont'd) personnel. Then there is the weather! A conflict of priorities about labour arises when pre-commissioning
wants equipment dismantled immediately after construction has
just finished its assembly. It actually makes sense to wel-
come the pre-commissioning team, they act as a checking function and try to keep equipment, pipe internals and electrics
clean and thus maintain a tidy site, not always constructions
first consideration. Of course, they annoy the Resident
Manager. These people not only want labour, plant and tools,
transport, office space, they want food and accommodation and,
even worse, they criticise! So an overall co-operative team
spirit must prevail if the desired Company objective is to be
achieved.

ACCEPTANCE CERTIFICATES

1. Fortunes vary dependent upon clients and their needs
what kind of a Provisional Certificate one may receive. If
the plant commissions smoothly, if the end product is required,
if the feed stock is available, if the Operator has a trained
operating team ready, one might receive a certificate with few
reservations. If, however, the Operating Manager will not
accept the plant from his Construction Manager, for whatever
reasons, then the list might be very long indeed. Generally,
contracts are precise on this aspect, everything shall be new
and complete. Lists of reservations can be long if the
clients work to contract. Painting and insulation are rich
fields for criticism, small bore piping needs supports, hand-
wheels are always missing, bolts extend or not beyond nuts.
If the client decides to retain a construction team on site,
one cannot walk off. The financial and contractual consequences will resist this. It is better to allocate a small
team to apply themselves and set to clear as many as
possible. Generally, providing the plant operates, a financial compromise will be agreed and the Certificates finally
issued. As most overseas Turnkey Projects compel the
contractor to issue Bonds or Bank Guarantees, it is unwise
not to co-operate and complete outstanding responsibilities.

CONCLUSIONS

1. Up to the late 1960's, most contracts were negotiated on
a Turnkey basis. It is during the last fifteen years that the
"Reimbursable" form of contract has become the vogue. The
reasons given are that projects have become very large, they
need client involvement, labour problems are more difficult,
Contractors must be Managing Contractors and sub-let construction work to smaller companies. These may be good and necessary reasons but they have probably increased the end cost of
projects.

2. A successful Turnkey Project requires an integrated team
dedicated to resolving the problems quickly and efficiently.
The design team must consider site problems and construction
methods available to the site. The senior site staff must be

CONCLUSIONS (CONTINUED)

2. (Cont'd) of prime concern to ensure working harmony. Financial terms are usually negotiated at Head Office and it is important that Personnel Departments are fully informed of the real site conditions and explain them accurately to those concerned. Nothing caused more trouble than overselling the site.

3. If the site conditions allow it, a working week of 6.1/2 days per week is better than 5, six is probably the minimum assuming that overseas sites can be in pretty bleak locations.

4. The back-up from Head Office must not only be, but must be seen to be good. Senior Head Office Management should visit site regularly, not only to see for themselves, but to reassure the site team that their progress is a matter of real concern to the 'office'. Special milestone achievements can be used as a good reason to lay on something special which generates good site relations.

5. Consideration must be shown to local employees, their voluntary co-operation be obtained for unfairness quickly circulates. This in no way implies that any relaxation of the rules is necessary, an equally costly attitude.

6. Though JBE&C's overseas projects have been technically successful with clients satisfied with the plant, they have not been financially very successful. Nevertheless, the Company realises that this is now the road we must pursue and is striving to put this hard gained experience to more profitable ends.

6 Joint ventures—formation and operation

J. A. ARMITT, John Laing International Ltd, London

SYNOPSIS.   The paper looks at the reasons for establishing a
Joint Venture, the care needed in partner selection and the
development of different types of Joint Venture.   The prebid
tender agreement, the final agreement, management structure
and modes of operation are all discussed with the objective
of providing guidelines for successful Joint Venture formation
and operation.

INTRODUCTION

1. The term Joint Venture is one which is heard with
increasing frequency in the construction business; not only
for overseas work but projects in the UK as well.   Often it
is seen as a panacea for winning work and for reducing risk.
Certainly there will be occasions when it will provide a
tender proposal with extra edge and a trouble shared can be a
trouble halved.   However, if a JV has been entered into without full consideration of all the issues, then its weaknesses
will likely be exposed precontract by the client, resulting in
no award, or worse at the execution phase, with consequent
problems for all concerned.

2. A Joint Venture is not the easiest form of association to
set up, manage and operate.   Before assuming a JV is the
appropriate way forward, managers should examine the more normal
way of combining skills through subcontracts.   In a subcontract
the responsibilities, liabilities and methods of payment are
well established and clear, whilst the cost of administration
is also probably less.

WHY A JOINT VENTURE?

3. What then are the arguments for adopting a JV approach?
Some typical reasons are:
To increase the credibility of a prequalification or bid by
demonstrating a predetermined commitment of the resources of
two or more companies.
To reduce exposure on very large projects to more manageable
proportions.
Combination of general resources.
Combination of specialist skills.
Sharing of bonding requirements.

Requirements for local participation (this is increasing as a reason).

Pride of individual partners which precludes subcontract.

'Some of the cake is better than none' attitude.

4. It will be seen that nearly all these reasons reflect either risk or size, except in the case of local requirements or where technology transfer is a separate objective.

5. The first question managers should ask is:

Can we prequalify for, and then execute, this job ourselves with subcontractors?

If the answer is 'no', it will be for one of several reasons. A close analysis of these reasons will identify the weakness and what needs to be done to remove the weakness. This will then assist in identifying the most suitable partner(s).

6. If this stage of the decision process is done thoroughly and logically, the basis for the Joint Venture should be sound. Also, if everyone understands why they are in the Joint Venture it will help in deciding what form it should take.

JOINT VENTURE TYPE

7. There are several types. However, most will fall into the broad categories of integrated and non-integrated. In the integrated form, the parties agree upon the proportions of financial participation and then combine their resources at all levels to complete the project.

8. In the non-integrated or decentralised form, the overall responsibility will lie with the Joint Venture, probably acting through a board. The Joint Venture, having negotiated and obtained the contract, will then subcontract to the separate sections of the contract; each partner being responsible for the technical and administrative elements of his work. Between the two extremes can clearly lie a variety of options.

9. In favour of the non-integrated approach is the situation where the partnership has been formed to complement skills. In such a situation the participation could well be unequal and the work may divide itself timewise - design, foundations, building, plant/M&E installation, commissioning.

10. The management of such a Joint Venture can be difficult; the need for mutual support being offset by the desire of each partner to succeed particularly in his sector. The representation of claims could also be awkward.

11. Another occasion when the non-integrated approach is favoured is where the parties do not have unreserved confidence in one another and therefore, prefer that each stands his own corner. If such a lack of confidence is at all marked, then the golden rule must be 'abort' before you start.

12. Conversely, the integrated approach is clearly favoured where it is difficult to split the work, or the project is so complex that it demands a highly structured and authoritative central management.

13. Remember also that the integrated version is less likely to lead to inter-company rivalries and should ensure maximum utilisation of resources, e.g. plant, staff and money.

14. Obviously an important factor is how many companies will be involved and, again obviously, the greater the number the more difficult will be operation of the venture.

15. It has been said that 'with more than three partners, the time spent consulting and trying to reach consensus will leave no time actually to do the work'.

16. Of course, this need not be the case, but certainly beware of large unwieldy Joint Ventures.

17. Another aspect of the form of Joint Venture is whether or not it is to be an incorporated company or an unincorporated venture governed by the agreement between the respective companies.

18. As you might expect, there are advantages and disadvantages to each course.

19. The incorporated company may be able, through local participation, to enjoy a tax holiday; it may be able to limit its liability to its share holding; it could have more status; the employment of staff and labour is more tidy.

20. Conversely, it will have the restrictions of Annual General Meetings; accounts will be less able to take advantage of capital allowances; it is more difficult to wind up.

PARTICIPATION

21. Once the partners have decided on the type of joint venture, they will then need to decide on the level of individual participation.   In other words, the various proportions in which they put in capital, provide staff and plant, support bonds, take profit and accept the obligations of the Joint Venture.

22. Participation does not need to be on an equal basis, but clearly to avoid internal strains at a later date the partners should feel that each is bearing a sensible proportion, taking into account the financial commitment that each is willing and able to put in, as well as the operational services provided, such as staff and plant.

23. At the same time as agreeing participation, the question of a JV sponsor or leader needs to be resolved.   Who should be sponsor can often be quite obvious in that one of the partners has a larger share, is the possessor of the particular skills central to the project, or has a special relationship with the client.   What is very important is that the duties the sponsor will undertake and the limits of his power and authority must be clearly set out when drawing up the JV to avoid misunderstandings and acrimony at a later date.   The more the sponsor undertakes by way of administration and management, the more the other parties will be inclined to be suspicious and critical, particularly if his additional costs are being directly reimbursed, rather than paid as a fee.   If the JV shares are equal, then it is probably better not to have a sponsor but to appoint a JV management team controlled by the JV board.

PREBID AGREEMENT

24. It is sensible at this stage to refer to the preliminary or prebid agreement.   To put together a full JV agreement can be a protracted affair.   For every company, allow at least one interested lawyer.   Put several of those in the same room and a definite deadline must be imposed if consensus is to be obtained.

25. However, the client is looking for an immediate commitment with the tender, or even at prequalification stage, whilst equally the prospective partners need to be assured that they are bound to one another.   Therefore, some form of preliminary agreement is required.

26. It need only be a short document but ideally should set out:
The partners.
The participation.
The sponsor (if appropriate).
Commitment to the project.
How tender costs will be split.
Basis of withdrawal.
An exclusivity clause binding the parties to the JV and preventing them from participating in other ventures or bidding for the work independently.
If possible (but not essential) a specimen JV agreement should be appended to indicate what type of document will eventually be entered into.

MANAGEMENT

27. Once an agreement in principle is reached, and assuming the JV has prequalified, the need for effective management through the tender period and beyond arises.

28. A joint venture is, whether incorporated or not, a mini-company and requires, therefore, a similar structure.

29. Typically the principle decision making group would be a management board or committee composed of one representative from each of the partners, together with a designated alternate. From hereon I will refer to this group as the 'Board'.

30. Reporting to the Board would be a general manager, appointed by the Board and responsible to them for operating the JV.

31. There will be a need for right of appeal in the event of strong disagreement on the Management Board and this can be to the Chairmen or Managing Directors of the respective partners, who may themselves form a small policy board which meets infrequently to review overall progress and performance.   Such a system is important because disagreements of this nature are unlikely to be suitable for settlement by arbitration.

32. What is of prime importance on the Management Board is that those on it must be sufficiently senior, with the authority to commit their companies to the policy decisions which will arise without the need to refer back.

33. There will, of course, be many legal and financial matters to be considered by the JV Board and separate groups

of specialist advisers should be identified to provide advice
to the General Manager and JV Board.

TENDER

34. The tender period will provide the first test of relationships in the JV. Tender management is always important
but in a JV especially so. This management should either be
the General Manager or a Bid Manager, specially appointed and
recognised by the Board.

35. The first decision to be made is how are the different
elements to be priced. Is the project to be split up with
each partner taking a section appropriate to his special skills,
or is everyone to price the whole job and then comparisons made
to find the optimum bid?

36. If time allows and it is a first bid for the JV, then the
latter approach may be best. It will ensure a cross flow of
experience and ideas, help to avoid recriminations at a later
date, and ensure total involvement of all parties.

37. However, as was recognised at the outset, JVs are often
formed for major projects, and size and time available may well
dictate a splitting of the estimating workload.

38. If this is the case, then early agreement will be needed
on common rates, e.g. labour and staff costs, whilst a co-ordin
-ated approach, preferably with common documentation, to sub-
contractors and suppliers is vital. Confusion will soon
reign if three or four partners are each approaching the same
supplier about the same or different elements of a project.
At the same time, optimum discounts will need to be assured.

39. During the tender, regular meetings must be held by the
bid manager to ensure a cross flow of ideas and to avoid any
partner travelling too far on a particular approach which may
be unacceptable to his partners.

40. However the price is being put together, do not under-
estimate the time which will be required to finalise the bid.
At least two weeks before submission, the first attempt at
putting the price together will be necessary. Despite the
best intentions, this will reveal differences in approach,
elements which have been overlooked altogether and technical
decisions which partners have made which will require agreement.
Overall preliminaries will need to be reviewed and, following
such a meeting, all partners will have revisions to adopt.

41. Presentation is another area which requires early agreement so that special printing of folders, letterheads, etc. can
be arranged.

42. The tender should be settled by the JV Board to ensure
that all members support the price.

43. This meeting will probably produce the first example of
'group think'. 'Group think' is a danger to any organisation,
and particularly to Joint Ventures. In essence, a particular
idea or approach is seized upon and each partner, determined
to show that he is as capable of entrepreneurial or conservative views as the others, increases the basis of the argument,
often well beyond the degree to which he would go in a free and
rational debate.

44. Many major decisions are taken in a JV during the tender stage and subsequently during project mobilisation. These decisions are taken at a time when the partners may still not understand one another very well. It is a time when they are being careful to develop a team spirit and not to rock the boat.

45. The result is that they may hold back on their real feelings, dilute them to appear reasonable, or be carried along by one member who is vociferous in his views. The results could clearly be disastrous and the sooner the JV Board has its first disagreement, which it them surmounts through full and frank discussion, the better.

46. All of this, of course, points to the need to have able and confident people representing each partner.

47. The other factor which the settlement meeting can often expose senior management to for the first time will be the real differences of business philosophy adopted by different companies. These can be increased if the partners are of different nationalities. Differences will arise, for example, on:

How to write down capital equipment.
Judgements on possible future buying gains.
How and when to take tax allowances.
Profit levels.
Methods of allowing overheads.
Treatment of seconded staff or labour.
Attitudes to welfare.
Management style.
Cash flow expectations.
Risk.
Contract conditions.
Qualifications.

48. Attitudes to all these will, of course, reflect the different partners' experience and the cross flow is clearly one of the benefits of working in a JV. However, partners must be careful not to be affected by only their most recent experiences and current vogues within their own company.

49. Conditions of contract which are unacceptable to an offshore partner may not concern a local partner, who has experience and knowledge of how such clauses will be interpreted.

50. What the settlement meeting will bring home to all concerned is that, in a JV, they are no longer totally masters of their own destiny. It is a lesson which must be quickly learned, because if individual members do insist on their corporate philosophies always being included, then a JV philosophy will be produced which will eventually become moribund and unwieldy. Compromise is required but must not be allowed to remove the cutting edge from decisions.

51. The submission of the tender will hopefully generate the first need for a JV negotiating body. Here the rules are no different to an ordinary contract; keep the team as small as is sensible; give the leader necessary powers; and try to use people who will have a continuing involvement in the project.

52. At the time the tender is submitted, it is clearly preferable, from an organisational and credibility aspect, that the formal Joint Venture document is agreed and signed; recognition being required, of course, that the contract negotiations may result in contract changes which must be reflected in the JV document.

53. I should now, therefore, like to dwell on the more important aspects of this document.

JOINT VENTURE DOCUMENT

THE RECITALS

54. Joint Venture agreements, in common with other legal documents, set out various pertinent matters, usually on the first page. Typically, reference will be made to the partners, the purpose for which the agreement is being made (e.g. the execution of the works) and the employer. A short description of the works and their location is also normally provided. This scene-setting preamble is known as the recitals and, while its form should not be of concern to managers, it is important to identify who are the actual partners.

GOVERNING LAW

55. Although this matter is usually mentioned at the end of the agreement, it will influence the whole format and nature of the document. There is no point in drafting or agreeing a document which turns out to be unenforceable. Therefore, the law by which the agreement will be interpreted must be designated before the legal draft is prepared. It should be noted that foreign law may impose a system upon the joint venture irrespective of what the joint venture agreement says. It is for the Joint Venture management to decide, after consultation with their legal advisers, which country's laws they wish to be governing. The governing law deals with the relationships between the partners and need not be related to the country of operation, to the country of the sponsor or any other partner.

REGISTERED OFFICE AND ADMINISTRATIVE HEADQUARTERS

56. Under English law an unincorporated Joint Venture is not a separate legal entity and there is no requirement to establish a registered office. Foreign systems differ, however, and local rules will need to be taken into consideration when determining whether or not to establish a registered office. Whatever is decided in this respect, the Joint Venture will naturally require administrative headquarters. Specialist advice should be taken when deciding in which country to establish these headquarters as, aside from purely logistical considerations, there are likely to be important tax implications.

NAME

57. The Joint Venture may find it advantageous to adopt a
title or style which can be registered as a business name if
necessary. When operating in foreign countries, care should
be taken to ensure that if some form of acronym is adopted,
it has no offensive or undesirable connotations!

SIGNATURE

58. In deciding who should sign the Joint Venture agreement
on behalf of each partner, it should be established that the
signatories are properly authorised to do so by the respective
company whose name appears in the recitals.

59. There may be certain tax and legal considerations to be
taken into account when deciding where and when the agreement
itself and other legal documents should be signed. Accordingly, the appropriate expert advice should always be sought
before signing. The agreement should specify who is
authorised to sign the contract.

DURATION

60. The agreement should specify when the Joint Venture
terminates, bearing in mind that it will continue to carry
certain obligations after the works are completed. The
agreement should take into account the possibility of partners'
liquidation, bankruptcy, dissolution, insolvency, etc. and
that the tender may be unsuccessful or rebid.

POWERS, OBLIGATIONS AND DUTIES

61. Having decided how the management of the Joint Venture
is to be effected, it is important to record what powers,
obligations and duties apply in respect of:
The Policy Board or Committee.
The Project Director or Manager.
The site management (if different from the Project Manager).
The sponsor.

62. Various aspects will need to be considered in respect of
each of these entities, e.g. frequency and venue of meetings,
quorums, minutes, decisions (how reached and recorded),
recruitment of staff, voting procedures, mechanisms for
resolving difficulties, method of electing chairman, etc. etc.

63. Furthermore, it should be stated that none of the
partners acting individually can commit the Joint Venture as
a whole unless the management board has vested the appropriate
authority in the partner concerned.

EXCLUSIVITY

64. The agreement should provide for a statement of exclusivity between the partners, similar to that mentioned above, in
the case of the preliminary agreement.

PROVISION FOR THE WITHDRAWAL OF PARTNERS

65. It should be recognised that a partner may find it
impossible to continue in the Joint Venture for various reasons.

This eventuality should be foreseen and provision made in the agreement for the remaining partners to assume the leaving partner's obligations, etc.

LIABILITIES OF PARTNERS

66. The liabilities of individual partners will depend on the Joint Venture agreement itself, the laws of the country of operation, the contract, whether the Joint Venture is integrated or not, and various other factors. In certain circumstances it may be necessary or desirable for the partners to waive their rights against each other or even to underwrite one another.

67. Alternatively, rights may be reserved, with each party indemnifying the others against its own negligence.

68. The employer, the national guarantee agencies and (possibly) the subcontractors will have an interest in whether the partners accept joint and several liability or several liability only.

69. This is a complex subject and legal and financial advice must be sought.

SPECIAL LIABILITIES OF SPONSOR

70. If sponsor company is appointed, does he accept liability for his performance in the exercise of his duties as sponsor?

LIQUIDATION AND RECEIVERSHIP

71. Careful provision will be necessary to recognise the involvement of a liquidator or receiver should the Joint Venture get into financial difficulties.

ASSIGNMENT

72. The assignment of rights and obligations to other companies should not be permitted without the agreement of the (none-involved) partners and, even then, not without some degree of control by them.

ARBITRATION

73. If an arbitration clause is included, its effect is that the ultimate body to whom conflicts, disagreements or disputes within the Joint Venture will be referred will be the arbitrator. Which person or body is chosen will depend on the contract, the nationality of the partners, and other factors. (In the absence of an arbitration clause, the ultimate body for resolving disputes will be the courts of the country of the governing law.)

REGISTRATION

74. Separate from the issue of whether the Joint Venture should or should not establish a registered office, the question of whether the Joint Venture should register as a business in the country of operation should also be considered. Consult financial controller and lawyer. By way of illustrating the

difficulties involved, an offshore Joint Venture aiming to operate in Nigeria must either register or apply for a certificate of exemption from registration. Unless one or other of these procedures is adopted, the Joint Venture will be unable to obtain work permits for its staff.

75. Theoretically, the Joint Venture has the option of forming itself into an offshore company, but this expedient is seldom used.

76. Hopefully we now have a Joint Venture which has been formed in the first place for sound business reasons with benefits to all partners, whilst they have formally bound themselves together with a document which recognises the main objectives, obligations of the partners and sets out a skeleton organisation. All that is now required is to operate the venture. Here the main principles which apply to any business are equally appropriate. However, with a Joint Venture several years are unlikely to be available in which to build up and achieve a smooth running organisation.

OPERATION

77. Because Joint Ventures normally relate to large projects and because companies recognise that their destiny is not wholly in their own hands, the ongoing operation of the Joint Venture will attract considerable attention.

78. Despite all the careful preparation, matters will arise which require policy decisions.

79. Therefore, in the first few weeks, it is sensible for the Board to meet every two weeks. During this period, policy decisions will be required on such matters as senior staff appointments, recruiting policy for labour, insurance, reporting procedures for physical progress and costs, valuations, financial accounts, client liaison policy, distribution of surplus cash, publicity, bank accounts, appointment of auditors, basis for recharges from partners, etc. etc. The reality of the authority required by the General Manager will also become clearer. It is no good telling the General Manager he must not spend more than half a million pounds on any order without Board authority and for the Board members to then disappear to the four corners of the globe.

80. During the early period, Board members will want and need to know what is going on in reasonable detail. It is likely that contact will be being made at different levels in the Joint Venture organisation, particularly as different specialist advisors become involved. The grapevine will be in full fruit. It is important, therefore, that the General Manager, ensures the same information is given out to all parties, that news of significant events is not allowed to trickle out in an adhoc manner and that responsibilities are clearly defined. The General Manager must also try to ensure that in appointing his team he gets a spread of people which reasonably reflects the level of partner participation.

81. This early period is very much about building up trust. No company can operate for very long if people do not trust one another's judgement and capability. If the Joint Venture is to settle down quickly into a united and purposeful group, then this trust must be rapidly established.

82. Clearly a key figure is the General Manager who must recognise this and consciously set out to bring all members of the team together. Equally the Board must trust the General Manager. He cannot manage if he is not given the authority and then made accountable.

83. Money spent on one or two social affairs at this time will be well spent.

84. A Joint Venture should live up to its title. It is the joint efforts and skills of several partners being combined in the most effective way to realise a project or projects.

7 Management contracting

J. R. ELTON, Bechtel Great Britain Ltd, London

SYNOPSIS.   Management Contracting covers a wide range of
differing roles and responsibilities. This paper gives
examples of the various forms of Management Contracting which
have been used together with their implications. The issues
involved in obtaining the advantages being sought are also
considered.

Introduction
        As projects in the construction industry, using the
terms in the widest sense, having become more complex, the
traditional approaches of clients using general contractors,
have been modified. The greater technical content, higher
capital cost and desire for shorter schedules has led to the
use of multiple contractors with specialised scopes of work.
Clients have also come to recognise that for certain projects
they can no longer manage their projects using only their own
resources.
        The experience gained from executing projects in these
changing circumstances has put pressure on those involved to
substantially improve the overall management, co-ordination
and planning activities in order to avoid cost and schedule
over-runs.
        This has led to the emergence of contractors providing
management services in support of clients involved in multi
discipline projects in which the Engineering, Procurement and
Construction phases generally overlap to optimise schedule and
cost. This role is variously described as Construction
Manager, Main Contractor, Management Contractor, Project
Management Contractor, and laterly in the Offshore Industry,
Project Services Contractor.
        In the search for improvement of the management function,
various approaches have been taken. This paper examines some
of these to show the wide variation in solutions available and
their implications.
        Each project, its scope, location and participants
involved will be different. Therefore there is no general
solution which can be applied "across the board". The project
management group responsible must carefully develop the management plan which includes the organisation and contracting plan
to meet the needs of the specific project.

Project Implementation

For a very large multi-discipline project many clients are unable to provide all the skills needed for the engineering, purchase of material and equipment, and the use of direct hire site construction personnel - even if this were the way to go.

It is also seldom the case that the client is prepared to pass the entire responsibility for the very large project implementation and hence, it's management to one single outside entity, e.g. the turnkey contractor.

The project management team and skills required will be different for each project and must be put together so as to provide highly motivated leadership. We are not talking about co-ordination with strong technical orientation but skilled management of engineering, procurement, construction supported by the tools of planning scheduling and cost tracking. This is increasingly coupled also with the need to be cognisant of legal issues, public relations, governmental regulations and media involvement stemming from industrial relations' problems and environmental considerations.

For success we must find the balance between too many participants involving too many interfaces, and the inevitable grey areas of responsibility, and the highly structured scenario with rigid boundaries so constrained that change is difficult to accommodate. Projects are subject to change - not only the much maligned "design change", but problems do occur which make material and equipment deliveries late, Industrial Relations' problems do occur at the construction site, soil surveys do miss the latent sub-surface hazard, etc. The attitudes of people and their organisations in this context are most important.

Do the participants see these as challenges to be met and managed to safeguard the project overall objectives, or mainly as potential excuses/claims for delay and increased cost? If the latter, this can produce the result that until these issues are resolved implementation of the required corrective action is inhibited to the detriment of the project.

To be successful, management of the multi discipline project must be led by an individual who is completely convinced of the project's viability and for whom it's success is a "cause celebre". This type of commitment has to come initially and continuously from the client. The client's project manager must decide how he can best be supported both from within his own organisation, and outside it.

At the outset the issues involved fall into two main categories:-

- o   Organisation of the Project overall
- o   Organisation to complete the "hands on" Engineering, Procurement, and Installation work

In dealing with these, the roles of the participants and the precise definition of these is vital.

The quality of the preparation will lay the grounds for success or failure.

Properly organised, the contractors' support becomes

part of a well structured integrated team with clear, mutually agreed objectives, taking on a task which can be seen to be achievable i.e. all can win.

Badly organised, interfaces are poorly defined - people find that they are expected to perform differently from their own perception of their role. Defensive attitudes arise leading to polorisation and ultimately an atmosphere of confrontation. A recipe for failure at worst; at best a feeling of "we got it done but at what cost" - both in financial and human terms.

So where are the points where client is directing, and where is he monitoring others using their skills on his behalf? How does the Project Management Team overall become established with mutually agreed and recognised objectives?

For many years supervision and management of projects was split using various combinations of consultants, architects, and contractors responsible for implementing construction, often involving managing other contractors/subcontractors in the field. Most of these arrangements split management of the overall project from the management of the design and construction phases.

Increasing project size, and the pressure to shorten project schedules, led to incidence of interface overlap and/or "black holes" with gaps in responsibility. Problems stemming from the inherent contractual barriers occurred, and a consistent project management approach was not provided throughout all phases of the project. Out of these problems has grown the use of Management Contract and Contractor with differing roles and responsibilities.

Examples of "Management Contracts"

In the charts shown below, the full lines represent the contractual relationships and the dotted lines, day to day interfaces for project implementation:-

1. Management Contractor (Building Industry).

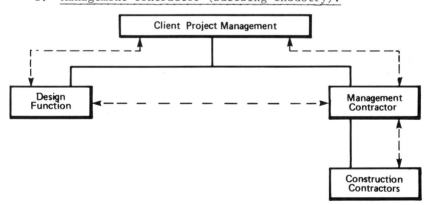

Client carries out overall project management but in this case the project is constructed by using multiple construction contracts let and managed by the Management Contractor with the approval of the Client.

2.   Construction Management Contractor.

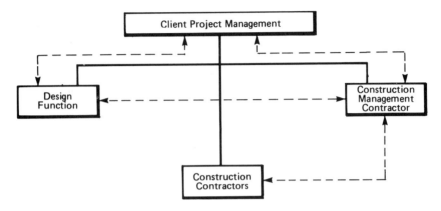

Client carries out overall project management but in this case the project is constructed using construction contracts let by the client direct with the contractors.   The Construction Manager, carries out overall management of the construction phase only acting for the client.

3.   Design and Management Contractor.

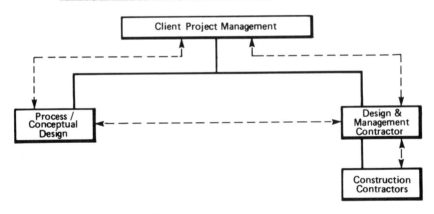

In this case client passes to the Design and Management not only the construction but the detailed design and engineering which has to be developed using conceptual designs which the client has established.

4.   Process Plant Engineering, Procurement, Construction Contractor (E.P.C.).   When dealing with process plants client may establish the plant conceptual design, and to reduce the construction phase duration procure long lead items.   He will then let contracts for the detailed engineering, bulk material procurement and construction to a contractor who will then manage and execute this work to meet client overall objectives for the project using his own resources and/or those of sub-contractors.

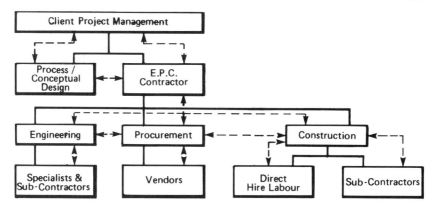

Clients hence may vary the Contractor element of the project depending on their own expertise and resource availability.

Clients will have a group of their own project management personnel monitoring the execution of the work by the Contractor and providing the approvals, etc., required by the Contractor from time to time.

The Contractor is responsible for the management and execution of the work within his scope to meet the overall project objectives set by the Clients project management group.

5. <u>Project Management Contractor.</u>   In this case the client appoints contractors to carry out "hands on" work, but uses a Project Management Contractor to manage the project on his behalf.

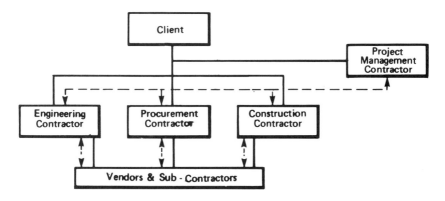

The project management contractor provides the overall project management organisation and personnel and manages the contractors on behalf of the client, although the contracts are directly between client and the contractors and/or vendors/subcontractors.

6. <u>Project Services Contractor</u>. Here the Client retains
the project management but uses the project services contractor
to compliment his own resources where this is needed. Thus the
Contractor and Client produce one fully integrated project
management team.

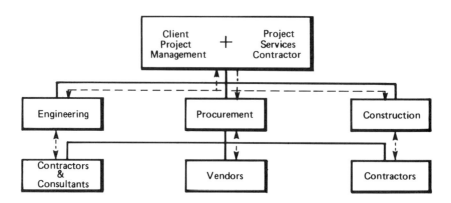

The above examples are typical and will be varied from
project to project to meet specific needs and circumstances.

<u>Roles of Client and Management Contractor</u>.
When using management contracting the organisational
and hence the contractual relationships will be significantly
different from those in the traditional situation if the
required advantages are to be gained. The advantages being
looked for are:-
o   Client is supplementing his own management resources and
    skills by use of those of the contractor.
o   Consistent definition and implementation of the project
    objectives by one management team over the life of the
    whole project.
o   Client and Contractors are one team with one goal – the
    success of the project. An adversarial climate is bad for
    the client, bad for the contractor and bad for the job.
o   The project management structure and manning can be
    tailored to the project needs utilising the complimentary
    skills existing in Client and Contractor personnel to the
    fullest extent.
o   An ability to respond in a controlled way to changed
    project requirements demanding flexibility, fast responses,
    and prompt decision making.
    Meeting these objectives requires the project management
team to become a self contained group acquiring it's members
from functional groups from various organisations and groups
outside it. Thus it has to operate in a matrix environment.
This must be accepted by the corporate managements involved
and be supported accordingly.
    For the full benefits to be gained from the use of

Management Contractors the project management group must be so established and located that not only is it a unified team on paper but is so located physically.

Very often on large projects it will be necessary to designate members of the team to be responsible for discrete parts of the project, and locate these in the offices/plant of the major contractors involved.

For the use of Management Contracting to be most effective the "Manager" should be appointed as early as possible in the life of the project. This enables the management group to establish its working relationships and procedures so that all concerned "buy into" the objectives and plans for the project as they are made and are thus committed fully to them. As has already been stated very careful attention must be given to the definition of the role of the Client and Management Contractor.

The respective roles typically cover the following activities:-

Client:
o   To define the project
o   To establish the objectives to be met to make the project successful
o   To provide decisions, approvals
o   To ensure the provision of adequate funding
o   To define who does what, and who monitors who
o   To ensure a site is available

In developing the "who does what" list the following major headings need to be considered and statused:-
o   Feasibility Study
o   Project Funding
o   Project Plan of Execution
o   Conceptual Design
o   Engineering and Detailed Design
o   Evaluation of potential equipment suppliers
o   Evaluation of potential contractors/sub-contractors for Construction and specialist services
o   Procurement plan
o   Project Planning/Estimating/Budgetting
o   Project Cost Control
o   Project Schedule Control
o   Accounting Procedures
o   Construction Plan
o   Industrial Relations Policies at Sites
o   Commissioning and Start Up Plan
o   Quality Assurance Programme

The Management Contractor:- The "hands on" entities must retain full responsibility for their function be it Engineering and Design, Procurement, or Construction/Start Up. However, those carrying out the work must be prepared to accept input from the Managing Contractor on the Client's behalf. All participants including Client must accept that the Management Contractor's role will demand that he pushes for decisions, requires prompt and in some areas detailed reports, and challenges assumptions on occasions.

All concerned must see this as a constructive contribution to the success of the project not a form of second guessing or point scoring, or merely the dotting and crossing of procedural "I's" and "T's". In this context it has to be borne in mind that the Managing Contractor may be managing or monitoring a competitor of his. Thus the rules of the game must be spelled out and enforced by the Managements involved. For his part, the Contractor must provide personnel capable of working in this scenario, having the qualifications and experience to be seen to bring the required additional expertise to the project. If the role is properly established and he provides the right quality of experienced personnel, the management contractor can be accepted by all concerned as a necessary catalyst or bridge builder, enabling problem definition and solution to be carried out speedily and with consistency over all the project activities.

Generally his role will include the tasks of programming, administration and monitoring of schedule and cost against the plan and budget for the project overall.

The extent to which he will carry out/supervise/monitor engineering and design, procurement, construction, quality assurance/control programmes will depend on the scope of the project, and the availability of Client resources.

The services typically included in the role of the Management Contractor can include the preparation and administration of the following:-

1. Project Management
o   Overall Project Planning, Estimating, Budgetting
o   Schedule Control
o   Cost Control
o   Evaluation of Project Options
o   Location of Project Home Office
o   Project Procedure Manuals
o   Claim Evaluation
o   Project Funding
2. Engineering
o   Drawing Control
o   Requisition Control
o   Vendor Information Control
o   Specification Review
3. Procurement
o   Purchase Plan
o   Contract/Sub-contract Plan
o   Preparation of Bidders' Lists
o   Preparation of Purchase Orders
o   Formulation of Contract Packages
o   Procurement/Delivery Status Reports
o   Expediting Reporting
o   Inspection Reports
o   Delivery Logistics
4. Construction
o   Construction Plan

o Contract/Sub-contract Plan
o Plan for, and provision of Temporary Facilities
o Contract and Sub-contract Administration
o Construction Scheduling and Cost
o Construction Progress Reporting
o Material Received Reports
o Conduct of Site Progress/Co-ordination Meetings
o Industrial Relations - establishment of policies and
   monitoring of claim procedures
   5. Finance & Administration.
o Payment of Project Accounts
o Cash Flow estimates for draw down from Project Funds
o Administration of Insurance Procedures
o Administration of Contractor invoice approval and Payment
   procedures
o Letters of Credit Administration
   6. Quality Assurance.
o Production of Project Quality Assurance Plan
o Production of Quality Assurance and Control Manual and
   Procedures
o Supervision/Monitoring of Quality Control

Liability and Risk Sharing

As has been stated earlier the use of Management
Contractors requires different contractual arrangements from
those traditionally used.

If confrontation and the adversarial syndrome is to be
avoided, roles and responsibilities must be clearly defined
and understood. The contract wording should be specific and
unambiguous minimising the possibility of differing inter-
pretations.

Where the Management Contractor is not directly carrying
out engineering, procurement, or construction work the types of
responsibility, liability and risk accepted in the traditional
contract are not appropriate. Client and contractors have to
share the risks between them differently.

The risk and liability carried has to be related to the
ability of those concerned to foresee, control, and make
reasonable provision for the issues involved, bearing in mind
the relationship of the financial liability involved to the
financial return expected on the contract. The contractor has
also to consider the summation of all risks he is having to
accept on his total contracts.

As the contractor's role moves away from "hands on"
execution towards provision of management services only the
further will his ability be reduced to accept traditional
responsibilities for defective work and other similar
responsibilities and liabilities.

The responsibilities, liabilities and risks which he
will be able to accept will be more akin to those associated
with professional consultancy. This is often a source of

misunderstanding stemming from failure to define and understand the variations in the role(s) sufficiently. The management contractor, leaving aside questions of any professional negligence, stands or falls by the quality of his work, it's results, and the reputation that this brings which directly affects his potential to win further work.

If a client decides to use a Management Contractor it has to be accepted that the pattern of risk sharing will be changed and can well leave the client exposed to more risk, although the overall risk to the project has not increased. In fact the likelihood of contingencies arising should be reduced since the object of using the contractor has been to improve the management of the project, in turn improving the performance on the project. This should reduce risk to the project of activities being completed incorrectly or not to schedule and budget. These factors plus the improved response to the neea to solve problems and make decisions should all lead to reduction in overall risk with its financial implications.

Payment

The contract agreeements for this type of contracting normally comprise a fee coupled with reimbursement of costs. When using this type of payment structure it is vital that the contract documents clearly define the following items:-
o   Directly reimbursable costs such as payroll costs, materials, etc.
o   Indirectly reimbursed costs to be reimbursed as an additive to the manhour costs.
o   Non reimbursable costs and profit deemed to be included in Overhead and Fee.

Advantages to be gained from Management Contracting

1. Client, by supplementing his own resources, with the wide experience and resources of the management contractor can establish a strong management group operating throughout all phases of the job.

2. Lines of responsibility are simpler.

3. The management group is able to provide speedy decisions based on valid and current data and its analysis.

4. With appropriate contracts and clear role definition the adversarial situation between client and contractors should be much reduced if not eliminated completely.

5. By breaking the project down into discrete packages, these can be procured and/or installed progressively so that the engineering, procurement and construction phases can be overlapped with resultant shortening of overall schedules.

6. Input at design phase of construction i.e. facility constructability, positioning and design of temporary facilities and services etc.

7. More realistic planning of construction drawing issue, material availability, etc.

8. Improved continuity of working throughout the life of the project.

9. Improved performance in cost and schedule control.

To maximise achieving these gains, attention must be given to the following in selecting the type of Management Contracting to be used.

1. The roles and responsibilities of Client and Contractor must be clearly defined and understood at the outset.

2. Choice of staff must be such that the project management group is a truly integrated one, that the members have the required experience/credibility and are compatible.

3. Apportionment of responsibility, liability and risk is consistent with the roles being assumed.

Acknowledgement

The author wishes to acknowledge the reference that has been made in the preparation of this Paper, to research and information contained in the Construction Industry Research and Information Association Report 100, 1983, entitled 'Management Contracting'.

8 Can the contract help?

G. L. JAYNES, Whitman and Ransom, London

An equally appropriate title for this paper could have been "Can we help the contract?" The contract is the text of the script from which the drama of an international construction project is to be played. Increasingly during the last decade, that script has been written around a plot which calls for the design and the construction to be done by the same contractor, and often for the design to be done concurrently with the construction.

When the performance of the script has not been what the scriptwriter planned, the reviews have been scathing. Can the contract help? Could some play-doctoring result in a better script, and enable the cast to produce a better performance? Or, as suggested above, "Can we help the contract?"

Whether the script calls for design before construction or design during construction, whether the cast includes an independent person or an employee of the Employer in the role of the Engineer, whether the script calls for a remeasured contract or a "turnkey" contract, one finds more often than not that the script is based on the Conditions of Contract (International) for Works of Civil Engineering Construction, known as "the FIDIC Conditions". The FIDIC script likely is familiar to you, as it now is in its Third Edition. First produced in 1958, it enjoyed a Second Edition, with no changes in the text, and not until it was nineteen years old was it revised, when the Third Edition was published in March 1977. Nearly eight years later, that Third Edition is still the current edition.

As with the First Edition, the Third is based upon conditions of contract published by this Institution. The Third Edition of the International conditions is based closely upon the Fourth Edition of the Institution of Civil Engineers Conditions of Contract. Members of the Institution played important roles in the creation of the Third Edition of the FIDIC Conditions.

Management of international construction projects. Thomas Telford Ltd, London, 1984.

As with the First Edition, the Third is based upon conditions of contract published by this Institution. The Third Edition of the International conditions is based closely upon the Fourth Edition of the Institution of Civil Engineers Conditions of Contract. Members of the Institution played important roles in the creation of the Third Edition of the FIDIC Conditions.

Undoubtedly one reason for the widespread use of the FIDIC Conditions is their approval by FIDIC, which has as members some thirty different national organisations of consulting engineers, plus their approval by some fifty-six different organisations of construction contractors from some fifty countries.

Based on the ICE Conditions, the FIDIC Conditions envisage the presence of an independent Engineer, who has prepared (prior to the FIDIC Contract): a set of drawings suitable for construction ("The Drawings"); a technical specification ("The Specification") suitable for fixed pricing of the work reflected in The Specification and The Drawings, a Bill of Quantities encompassing all of the work to be performed; and, perhaps, a Schedule of Rates and Prices so that with the combination of Bill and the Schedule, the work to be done throughout the term of the Contract is almost completely priced at the time of signature of the Contract.

Seldom does one see a major project in a developing country in which these intended parts of the FIDIC Contract are in fact available in the way contemplated by the drafters of the FIDIC Conditions. It is more common to find that if there is an Engineer, he is only an advisor to the Employer and not independent as between the Employer and the Contractor, The Drawings are little more than conceptual, and one of the duties of the Contractor, subject to the review and approval of the Engineer, is the detailing of those drawings to a level suitable for construction. The Specification is sketchy and may be comprised of data submitted by the Contractor with the Tender, amounting to little more than an equipment list. There is no Bill, nor is there a Schedule of Rates and Prices. Nor will the Conditions of Contract have been used in the way their drafters intended: whatever criticism one may have of the FIDIC Conditions, at least they reflect an effort to achieve a balance of interests. Such an effort seldom is reflected in the Conditions of Contract typically put to tender in major international projects today.

So, having taken a script written for a different drama, and having revised that script to an extent which can only be termed distortion, is it any surprise that the players in the cast produce a performance different from that intended by the playwright?

86

For this reason, it is the thesis of this paper that there should be a new script for those projects for which both design and construction are the responsibility of a single Contractor -- the "turnkey" contract -- and that this new script should have a plot which allows for concurrent design and construction. Also, since this honorable Institution has a tradition of initiative in such matters, this paper urges that the Institution assigns to a group of its members the task of serving as playwright for this new script.

A team drawn from the Institution's members should draft conditions of contract designed to serve for such projects, and put that draft forward to FIDIC for its consideration. This should be followed by the necessary solicitations to colleagues in other member countries of FIDIC to assure that the project receives the support required to result in a FIDIC-proposed set of Conditions. This would be circulated to the other organisations who have approved the Third Edition of the FIDIC Conditions of Contract (International).

Such an enterprise would be of service not only to the profession of civil engineering but also to the construction industry in general, and to future Employers everywhere. Doubtless no form of contract ever will discourage completely amateur turnkey contract playwrights from trying their hands at excisions and additions, usually with lamentable results, but the script which emerges from such tinkering is more likely to suffice if the original script at least was created for projects requiring design and construction to be done by a single Contract.

This new script could take as its starting point the Third Edition of the FIDIC Conditions. If so, how would this new script differ from the Third Edition? It is submitted that there are two categories of differences to be considered. The first includes those differences which might be termed suggested improvements on the Third Edition. During the years since 1977, when the Third Edition was published, FIDIC has received suggestions for improvement from many sources, and has them under consideration in connection with a projected Fourth Edition. The Institution should liaise with FIDIC and review those suggestions as a preliminary to using the Third Edition as the starting point for the new script. The second category of differences includes those provisions of the Third Edition which necessarily must be revised to cater for the very different type of project for which the new script is intended.

If one may be a "pre-performance critic", one can suggest some provisions of the Third Edition which are in the second category, and require rewriting before use in the script. They include the following Clauses:

Clause 2, Engineer and Engineer's Representative

The concept of this Clause is that the Engineer shall have the power to make certain decisions, issue certificates, and issue orders, all as required by the terms of his appointment and set forth in Part II of the FIDIC Conditions. In addition, the Engineer's Representative is to supervise the Works and to test and examine materials and workmanship. The Engineer's Representative also may perform other of the Engineer's duties if empowered in writing by the Engineer. These are responsibilities one expects for what one might term the "classical" independent consulting engineer.

However, in turnkey projects, one seldom sees such duties vested in the Engineer, and usually the role of the Engineer is far from that of the classical independent consultant. Decisions, certificates, and orders are the domain of the Employer. The Engineer, if not actually a part of the Employer's organisation, is likely to be the loyal advisor of the Employer, and, as between Employer and Contractor, far from independent.

These facts must be kept in mind not only in any Clause 2 provision, but also in the many clauses throughout the FIDIC Conditions which give significant authority to the Engineer over the Contractor. Examples are the authority of the Engineer to determine the entitlement of the Contractor in the event of suspension of work (Clause 40), and in the event of occurrences fairly entitling the Contractor to extension of the time for completion of the Works (Clause 44), and to fix rates and prices for variations in the Works (Clause 52).

If the Engineer is not independent as between the Employer and the Contractor, he should not have such broad authority in these matters. Instead, such matters could be dealt with by the board we shall consider later, in connection with disputes settlement.

Clauses 6 and 7, and The Drawings

Because the FIDIC Conditions presume that the Contract Documents include drawings sufficient for construction, there are few provisions in the Conditions relating to drawings, and those Conditions are brief. Clause 6(3) sets a procedure for the Contractor to follow if the Contractor anticipates delay or disruption in the planning or progress of the Works unless a drawing is forthcoming from the Engineer within a reasonable time, and this sub-clause also foresees an equitable adjustment to the Contract if the Engineer fails to act. Clause 7 empowers the Engineer to supply to the Contractor, during the progress of the Works, "...such further drawings...as shall be necessary for the purpose of the proper and adequate execution...of the Works. The Contractor shall carry out and be bound by the same."

But things do not happen that way on turnkey projects. The responsibility for timely completion of design is on the Contractor. Also, the responsibility for adequacy of the design is on the Contractor. Nevertheless, it is usual for the Employer to have the Engineer review and approve the design of the Contractor, and to have the Engineer assist the Employer in deciding whether any changes in the proposed design should be required of the Contractor. Thus, it is the Contractor who is supplying the drawings, not the Engineer, although the drawings likely are reviewed and approved by the Engineer.

A further consideration arises in most turnkey contracts: usually the Contractor's design team will be elsewhere than in the country of the project, and often will not be in the same country as the Engineer. This can lead to a three-cornered path for the review and approval of design, with documents being shuttled among three countries -- the Employer's, the Engineer's and the Contractor's -- before they are finally approved and in the hands of the Contractor's workforce at the Site.

Experience suggests that the Contract should contain detailed procedures for this process, including a stipulation of the time allowed for the Engineer's review (with due allowance for the transportation of documents between countries), and similarly for resubmittals pursuant to revisions requested by the Engineer. A detailed programme for the design work should be submitted by the Contractor, approved by the Engineer, and agreed with the Employer, and delays arising due to reviews exceeding allotted times, or due to portions of design being placed on "hold" by the Engineer or Employer, should give rise to equitable adjustments to the Contract, in the same manner as would be the case if the Engineer or Employer issued Variation Orders requiring changes in the Contractor's design. The graveyard of unsuccessful or delayed projects is studded with tombstones testifying to the fact that programming and timely completion of the design portion of a turnkey contract is equally as important as the planning and completion of the construction portion.

Clause 11, Inspection of Site

The intention reflected in this Clause is that the Employer shall have included in the Tender documents data on hydrological and sub-surface conditions, obtained from investigations previously undertaken. The Contractor is to make his own interpretation of such data, and assess its significance to his Tender, including his pricing. His only relief in this respect is under Clause 12, in the event that during construction he encounters physical conditions or artificial obstructions which could not have been foreseen by an experienced contractor.

Referring again to the role of the "classical" consulting engineer, formerly this usually would have included the conduct of the investigations necessary to obtain the data included in the Tender documents. The scope of such investigations would have been sufficient to satisfy the consultant that he had the data required to prepare the design of the project.

In part due to pace at which developing countries seek to execute their projects (and, therefore, employ turnkey contracts) these investigations seldom have been taken to the point that a professional engineer would consider the data in hand sufficient to complete the design. Further investigation often is one of the Contractor's initial tasks. The Clauses in our script should recognise this, and should provide that if the Contractor's investigation discloses conditions which, at the time of Tender, could not have been foreseen by an experienced contractor, then the Contract will be equitably adjusted in light of the results of the investigation.

Clause 15, Programme to be Furnished

This Clause provides that whenever the Engineer considers that the progress of the Works is not in accordance with the original programme, the Engineer may require the Contractor to submit a revised programme. However, in a turnkey contract, the Engineer may have great difficulty in assessing the progress of the Works, especially before work begins at the Site, because the Engineer's involvement in design is peripheral, and because in turnkey project arrangements, the Engineer frequently has no significant oversight of the Contractor's preparations prior to commencement of construction at the Site.

The Institution's scriptwriters should consider imposing the initiative for programme revisions upon the Contractor, with not less than monthly revisions of a detailed programme showing the status of design as well as the status of construction. In a complex project, not less than weekly updates of a Critical Path Method programme are appropriate, including (or accompanied by) a report of the status of the Contractor's procurement programme. These programming arrangements should be detailed in the Conditions of Contract, and preferably supplemented with sample forms for use in programming, all supplied with the Invitation to Tender.

Clause 51, Alterations, Additions and Omissions

This Clause, often termed the "Variations Clause" is the vehicle for the ordering of changes by the Engineer or the Employer. In a contract structure calling for the Contractor to prepare the design, the scriptwriters should consider restructuring this Clause to deal with design changes requested or proposed by the Contractor, not just those

required by the Employer. Such provisions avoids suppression
of the turnkey contractor's incentive to propose design
changes advantageous to the project. Also, the scriptwriters
may wish to consider restricting the Clause to design
changes within the original scope of the Works. A separate
clause could be used to cover the Employer's alterations to
the original scope of work, whether by deletion of work or
addition of work. Such an additional clause might be
drafted with thought to the prevention of unfair use of such
power of addition or deletion.

Clause 60, Certificates and Payment
Both in Part I and in Part II of the FIDIC Conditions,
attention is directed to the mechanics of payment but no
attention is directed to two areas of major concern in
turnkey projects: project finance, and, the consequences of
delays in payment of the Contractor for reasons not the
fault of the Contractor.

Few international construction projects take place
today without bilateral or multilateral financing, and often
both are employed. Experience repeatedly has demonstrated
the importance of having the contract contain a clear
description of the financing arrangements as they relate to
payment, preferably with appendices containing sample
documents required for drawdowns against the project
financing.

The awesome monetary size of today's international
construction projects should alert us to the importance of
timely payment to the Contractor. Contractors seldom are
heavily capitalised, and significant delays in payments to
them can lead to crippling of progress, and of the
contractor, and ultimately even to crippling of the project.
However, the FIDIC Clause gives no relief for the Contractor
if such delays occur, other than the Clause 69 entitlement of
the Contractor to terminate his employment if the Employer
fails to pay within thirty days of the date payment is due:
hardly a satisfactory relief in a major international
project! The script surely should provide for compensation
to the Contractor for his damages in the event of such
delays, and enable him to slow down or even suspend work if
necessary.

Clause 67, "Settlement of Disputes"
It is rare to find this clause intact in a turnkey
contract. In large part, this is due to the understandable
tendency of developing countries to require that disputes
which cannot be resolved amicably be submitted to the
procedures of the country of the Employer, whether they be
procedures of arbitration, or of administrative agency
resolution, or of submission to the courts of the country.
We all are aware of the anxieties such provisions arouse
among contractors for whom the country of the Employer is a

foreign country, and with whose procedures for dispute resolution the Contractor has little, if any, prior experience.

Our already overworked scriptwriters may wish to consider providing for a board to be appointed at the time of contract and named in the contract, to serve as arbiters of disputes arising during the progress of the Works. This could avoid the Employer's aversion to international arbitration under foreign institutions and avoid the Contractor's fear of what for him are unknown and unfamiliar procedures in the Employer's country.

If the laws of the Employer's country do not permit any dispute resolution procedure to be binding in Government contracts except the procedure stipulated by law in the Employer's country, the decisions of this contractually appointed board could be without prejudice to the rights of either party under the applicable Government law regarding dispute resolution. Experience has shown that in many cases the parties accept such board decisions even though not legally bound to do so, and do not pursue the dispute any farther, notwithstanding their legal entitlement to do so under procedures established by the law of the Employer's country.

Clause 69, Default of Employer
This Clause envisions that little in the way of default of the Employer can arise except with respect to matters relating to payment of the Contractor. While every contractor certainly will consider payment the cardinal obligation of the Employer, our playwrights must consider that turnkey contracts usually take place in developing countries, and it is common for the Employer to undertake many other obligations which also are of great importance to the Contractor. Examples are: furnishing of materials available within the Employer's country, such as cement from a factory which has been built in the employer's country, relief from import duties, relief from taxation on income, assistance in obtaining visas for the Contractor's manpower; and the supply of manpower by the Employer for training by the Contractor. Where an Employer undertakes these obligations, it is important that the time for their performance be set forth in the contract, and that the contract provide that any delay in performing, or failure to perform, these undertakings shall give rise to an equitable adjustment to the contract.

* * * *

Many of you already will have thought of other FIDIC Conditions which require re-examination before use in turnkey contracts. The creative effort required to produce the script is imposing. As with any demanding task, few will rush to volunteer. But the Institution of Civil Engineers has risen to the challenge of comparable needs in the past, and is uniquely qualified to meet the need for this new script, so that the drama of international construction projects can be performed to greater satisfaction, especially for the players.

Can the Contract help? Most decidedly. Can <u>you</u> help the Contract? Most certainly. The need is evident. One rests with the Institution the plea that you do help, and without delay.

Discussion on Papers 5–8

MR A.R. PARISH, W.S. Atkins Group Consultants

I found Paper 5 of particular interest because at the time that John Brown were constructing the pipeline in the west of Algeria, my own company was heavily engaged with the steel works in the east. Taking account of the inevitable differences between the experiences of a contractor and consultant, it presented a very familiar picture.

The essence of a turnkey project is that to a very large extent the owner stands back and allows the contractor a reasonable degree of freedom to perform his contractual obligations. Today there is more emphasis on the transfer of technology to the owner's country and, at least at the level of technologists, this seems to be at variance with the basis of a turnkey project. Does Mr Donovan see this conflict as affecting the future use of turnkey projects?

MR DONOVAN

When letting major contracts, it is a growing practice for clients, having gone through a series of 'selection' meetings, to appoint one or more contractors to undertake a 'Preliminary Engineering Study' during which the process is optimised and major items of engineering hardware are specified, all with the active participation of the client.

This document, then, forms the basis of the subsequent tender for detailed engineering, procurement and construction. Thus, a turnkey project can be negotiated with many or most of the major issues resolved.

The contractor responsible for the engineering study, while 'enjoying' a clearer understanding of the project, does not necessarily win the contract, although clients do seek to limit claims by ensuring that all design is the responsibility of one contractor.

With smaller contracts, a client may well start engineering on some form of reimbursed basis, moving at an appropriate time to a fixed lump sum basis for completion of engineering, procurement and construction.

Thus I believe that this conflict of interests can be satisfactorily married.

MR SIBERRY

Few so called turnkey projects live up to the pure definition
and contractors must allow for an amount of client
'interference'. It helps at the final take-over if the
contractor has taken the client's technologists along with him
during the engineering development phases.

MR C. I. SIBERRY, John Brown Engineers & Contractors Ltd

With reference to Paper 6, I would first like to compliment
Mr Armitt on his Paper. There is little with which I can take
issue, but I wonder whether Mr Armitt's non-integrated joint
venture is worthy of the name, or is it in fact a consortium?
A consortium, as I understand it, is a group of companies who
agree to co-operate, with one company acting as manager, in
order to carry out a complete project, with each individual
company doing its own work, often for its own price. It is,
in effect, a collection of sub-contracts, with the overall
management expenses shared on an agreed basis and like a joint
venture, the companies usually have joint and several, or
several liability.

A consortium can have any number of member companies from
two upwards and can, in addition to member companies, have a
number of nominated sub-contractors who do not share liability
in the overall management. Consortia do not require the same
degree of trust between parties as joint ventures do, but, as
Mr Armitt has said, if there is marked lack of confidence
better 'abort before you start'.

Coming back to joint ventures, I would like to emphasise the
necessity for complete trust between the participants in any
true joint venture, the best of all types being, in
Mr Armitt's terminology, the integrated approach, or in the
jargon 'all in the pot'. In this type of joint venture the
management will be composed of the best people drawn from
both, or all, companies in the venture, and the first loyalty
of such staff must be to the venture. It is not always easy,
but if achieved the joint venture will be a success, even if
the particular project is not financially profitable. It will
inspire the partners to continue, and with growing experience
the venture must succeed.

MR CAMPBELL SCOTT, Taylor Woodrow International

I would comment on Paper 6, paragraph 26, on the danger of
assuming, in an international joint venture, that our partners
understand clearly the meaning and implications of the term
'Joint Venture', as compared to, say, 'Consortium and
Partnership'. The terms are often considered to be
synonymous. Further, one must examine whether the law of the
host country allows or restricts, the sort of joint and
several liability envisaged in our standard joint venture
wording.

I would suggest an addition to the requirements of
paragraph 65, to cover a statement of the <u>residual</u> obligations
of a failed or withdrawn partner.

Finally, would Mr Armitt please explain how he would handle the problem, in a multi-national joint venture, of differing salary and benefit packages paid to people doing the same job alongside each other, on account of their coming from different countries with different company benefit traditions?

MR ARMITT

I agree that a non-integrated joint venture may be called a consortium. The title is really immaterial. What is important is that all those concerned understand the relationship.

Certainly, any detailed clause referring to the departure of a joint venture member should recognise the possibility of residual obligations.

I do not think it would be wise to try to bring salaries into line. There will be good reasons why an engineer from, say, the UK is paid differently to one, say, from Italy. Each company should retain responsibility for its employees' payments. The consequent problems of bringing salaries into line would far outweigh any problems which might arise during the course of the joint venture agreement.

With regard to accommodation and cars, it would, of course, be sensible to try and ensure reasonable compatibility.

MR D.G. COMPSTON, Allott & Lomax

I think one should draw attention to the traditional roles of the consulting engineer and the contractor. The consulting engineer is primarily the designer, while the contractor is basically the constructor. Clearly, if these two skills could be harnessed into one team the chances for success would be greater. The consulting engineers have a great deal to offer, in the context of turnkey contracts and joint ventures, as the design members of the team, and they are frequently employed by turnkey contractors to undertake this function.

It has to be appreciated, however, that there is a significant problem at the tendering stage. Undoubtedly, turnkey contractors or joint venture organisations must offer the customer the best design concepts, incorporating features which ensure the completed project meets the customer's needs in the most economical way. Before the turnkey contractor can price his bid, he must have completed sufficient design work to be able to establish his price properly. While fully detailed design at this stage is totally out of the question, as there is not the time, nor would it be sensible to spend the money, it is still necessary to reach a stage which represents a significant proportion of the designer's total work on the project.

At the tender stage, the constructor is basically required only to price the work which is offered to him for construction. However, the designer is required not only to provide a price for the cost of the design work he will have to undertake, should the project go forward, but has also to do part of that design work during the tender stage.

Consultants naturally expect to quote prices they will charge for their services without commitment from their potential client, in this case the turnkey contractor, but can indulge in speculative design at the tender stage only to the extent that it is commercially sensible to do so in relation to the potential gain that they will achieve should the contract go ahead. It follows, therefore, that the contractor should be prepared to meet his share of the tender design costs as part of the speculative expenditure, bearing in mind that between 90-95% of the income from the contract will relate to the construction, while only between 5-10% will relate to the design. There is no doubt that experienced consulting offices can, at the tender stage, provide outline designs on which tenders can be based, on an economical basis, and they should be prepared to do so at minimum cost. However, it has to be recognised by all parties that the ultimate risk taking, in relation to the cost of the constructed works, can be carried only by the turnkey contractor who has the financial resources to back the venture, and who also stands to gain the most if the contract is profitable.

Consequently, the turnkey contractor must have full confidence in the outline design work done by the consultant at tender stage; and there must be a realistic appraisal by the turnkey contractor and the consultant, before the tender is finalised, of the extent to which the design development will affect the cost of the constructed works in order to ensure that the tender price makes provision for the work which cannot be shown in the outline design.

Provided that these principles are accepted and borne in mind, then great benefit will be derived from the involvement of consultants in turnkey and joint venture works.

MR M.A. AL-MUFTI, Queen's University, Belfast

With reference to Paper 7, could the Author briefly indentify areas of difficulty or disadvantage in the use of management contracts?

In the past, some developing countries have formed state companies for construction contracts or consultancy services. Does the Author think the same can be done with management contracting?

MR ELTON

First, with regard to areas of difficulty or disadvantage in the use of management contracts, such difficulties can arise for the following reasons.

1. The management contractor is not appointed early enough in the project to enable his personnel to be part of the decision making process during all stages of the project with which the contractor is concerned.
2. Inadequate consideration and definition is given to the role of the management contractor. In many cases, client

and contractor will be familiar with their more
conventional roles, but often insufficient attention is
given to the responsibilities and liabilities in the
management contracting relationship and the associated
contracts. This can be a particular cause of difficulty
in the area of quality assurance and control.

3. For the contractor, there is a need to ensure that in
    accepting management contracts there is a balance between
    these and conventional 'hands-on' contracting work to
    ensure utilisation and retention of all the resources
    needed to preserve a comprehensive contracting capability.
4. For the client, the use of a management contractor may
    produce an increased exposure to risk, although risk to
    the project as a whole should be reduced on account of the
    improved performance on the project which should result
    from the use of a management contractor.
5. There can be a tendency to produce increased
    administration and management/supervision costs, unless
    the structure and integration of the project management
    team is given careful consideration to avoid unnecessary
    duplication of roles and responsibilities which, in turn,
    leads to loss of direction and motivation for the project.

Second, can developing countries form state management
contracting companies? In principle, there is no reason why
this should not be done. However, its success will depend on
the ability to draw into the company, personnel of the
required experience and standing so that they can perform the
management role with recognised expertise and standing. If
this is not the case, the state management contractor will not
be able, nor be seen to be able, to make an effective
contribution to the project effort.

Like private contractors, the state contractor will have to
be aware that unless the capability to carry out 'hands-on'
work is also utilised, the management capability may become
isolated from current trends and practices, and thus become
less effective.

MR J.B.L. FAULKNER, W.S. Atkins Group Consultants
Papers 7 and 8 discuss just two of the many forms of
contract available for use on large international projects and
I want to follow up two aspects that have been raised,
reducing the conflict or adversary situations and increasing
trust.

How does the promoter of a project - the client - decide
which 'script', to use Mr Jaynes's word, he wants writing in
the first place? Has he enough experience and knowledge to
choose anyway? Many clients are fully capable of doing this,
but on the international scene, as so many Papers at this
Conference show, the client is relatively inexperienced,
unsophisticated and does not have any real understanding of
projects, the latter's behaviour and the implications of
different forms of contract.

It is part of the job of firms such as mine, in the consulting arm of the international projects business, to help a client in this situation. Our experience, both in project management and project audits, shows that the better and stronger the client, the better the job, so it is in everyone's interest that the advice we give is right. Naturally, we believe that it usually is, but it is certainly a different solution for each project. I would suggest that there are five main factors involved.

1. The client must fully understand his role and responsibilities, together with the advice he receives, the complexity of the task he is undertaking and the many personal and organisation inter-relationships that have to be set up and controlled.

2. He needs to have, as Mr Elton has rightly emphasised, a strong project management team, drawn either from his own resources or from external sources. This team must provide leadership, motivation and decisions.

3. The client has to be fully aware of the range of alternative forms of contract that are available. This, of course, ranges from the package deal or turnkey at one end of the spectrum, through the so-called conventional contracts, target cost, and management contracting to cost plus at the other end. What should be clear is that there is no 'best' or universal form of contract that can be applied, and that the pros and cons of using these various forms on the particular project concerned must be thought through. Too many overseas clients have suffered from the, what appears to them, natural attractions of turnkey.

4. For each type of contract, the client needs to understand the allocation of risks between himself and the contractor, and in doing so, he must fully absorb the advice he receives.

5. The client should have as his prime objective that of reducing 'conflict'. By the choice of the right form of contract and the correct allocation of risk, the origins of conflict on the project can be reduced with the positive benefits of establishing good relations between all concerned. As a result, everyone benefits by obtaining earlier and cheaper completion and increased return or profit. The main origins of such conflict are, in my view, as follows.

   (a) A lack of knowledge of project behaviour
   (b) The often large number of parties involved: consortium clients, joint venture contractors, etc.
   (c) The influence of outside parties, e.g. Governments, Safety Authorities, Planning Authorities, Pressure Groups, etc.
   (d) Lack of clear definition of requirements
   (e) Incorrect allocation of risks
   (f) Poor performance by client, consultant or contractor
   (g) The development of lack of trust between all concerned.

All of those in the international project business, whether
Government, Client, Financier, Consultant, Contractor or
Supplier, can, by proper understanding, reduce the degree of
conflict and produce a little more of that magic ingredient -
trust!

I would submit that the result would be better project
performance, more satisfied clients and therefore more work,
which we, as an industry, all need.

MR T.H. NICHOLSON, Consulting Engineer

With reference to Paper 8, I would like to make a plea for
the non-proliferation of types of conditions of contract.

Before we embark on the drafting of a new set of conditions
because we have found that the existing standard is
inappropriate in some respects for a particular style of
contract strategy, I suggest that we pause to consider what
the fundamental job of the conditions is within the totality
of a contract which, traditionally, is defined in five
documents:

1. CONDITIONS of Contract
2. SPECIFICATION
3. BILL of Quantities
4. Form of TENDER
5. Form of AGREEMENT

There are many variations of contract strategy for capital
projects, extending from the traditional admeasurement
construction contract for a design by the engineer, to a
turnkey with design and construction being the responsibility
of the Contractor. Is it necessary to have a different set of
conditions for each of these extremes (and if one does, what
about the intermediate variations?) or could we have a
contractual framework applicable to the whole range?

The latter approach has been successfully applied in
projects for industry in the UK, covering that range of
contract strategies and also all the engineering disciplines
plus building. The conditions used were a modified form of
the Institution's Fifth Edition, including two key amendments.

1. The term 'Bill of Quantities' clearly infers measurement
   and may not be appropriate. It was therefore replaced
   throughout the conditions by a new term, 'Schedule of
   Works', with the following definition:

   'Schedule of works' means the Schedule of Works referred
   to in the Memorandum of Contract and may include bills
   of quantities, daywork schedules, schedules of rates
   and/or schedules of lump sum items which, when priced by
   the Contractor at the date of acceptance of his Tender
   for the Works, shall provide the rates and prices, to be
   used in ascertaining the Contract Price.

   The Schedule, therefore, retained the Bill's function of
   setting out the methods and procedures by which the

Contract Price would be determined without restricting those methods to measurement. Explanations of the chosen method for a particular contract would be given in the preamble to the Schedule which is the appropriate document for relating a definition of the Works to how the Contractor will be paid for executing them.

2. The definition of 'Works' was extended as follows:

'Works' means the Permanent Works together with the Temporary Works and any design to be provided by the Contractor in accordance with the Contract.

The appropriate document for the description of the Works is the Specification which would include a definition of the Contractor's design responsibilities together with the design standards to be achieved. (This is normally necessary in any case in most traditional contracts in which the Contractor usually has some design responsibility, however small.)

These two key amendments to the Institution's Fifth Edition, together with other consequent changes affecting drawings by the Contractor, time for approval by the Engineer, Programmes for the Works (including design), methods of measurement (if any) etc., enabled the conditions to establish the legal framework for the range of contract types considered. A typical set of contract documents would consist of:

1. CONDITIONS of Contract
2. SPECIFICATION
3. SCHEDULE of Works
4. Form of TENDER
5. Form of AGREEMENT

The requirements for a particular contract would be defined in the Specification and the Schedule in accordance with their respective functions in the total contract as I have indicated.

I suggest that this approach should be given serious consideration for international work.

9 Training and involvement of overseas firms

M. R. STARR, Sir William Halcrow and Partners, Swindon

SYNOPSIS. Technology transfer has long been recognised as the key to establishing a greater degree of self-reliance in the developing world. The problem has always been how to achieve it. To be effective, a training programme needs to be developed from a careful analysis of the training needs and firmly based in the developing country concerned. Close involvement of overseas firms will provide not only specific skills but also local knowledge and longer term continuity. With good will and good planning, both the quantity and quality of the training provided as part of development projects may be significantly improved.

PLANNING THE TRAINING PROGRAMME

Overall objectives

1. Most major aid-funded development projects now include a requirement that the consulting engineers and contractors involved provide training for local personnel. The specific requirements vary, but often the need for on-the-job (OTJ) training is emphasised, supplemented by lectures and training courses. Increasing weight is being given to training proposals when offers are being evaluated, as is clear from recent World Bank and other development agency publications.

2. Technology transfer and training has sometimes been viewed with scepticism by consultants as being a frustrating complication which probably will not be effective anyway, but even if it is, will undermine their future work prospects. Fortunately, this attitude is changing as the requirements for appropriate training are better understood and it is appreciated that good training proposals can help secure new work.

3. The transfer of new knowledge and skills takes time and must take place in a context wider than that defined by the boundaries of the particular project being used as the vehicle for the training. We are really talking about the development of human beings, so that they can achieve their full potential in their professional sphere. Although it is tempting to raise expectations too high at the start of a training programme - "when we are finished in 18 months, you will be

able to take over" - it is nevertheless important that those for whom the training is intended become excited by the prospects and the challenge. So often the morale of professionals in the developing world is badly depressed by the (apparent) confidence and competance of the expatriates they are put alongside. Not only may there be language and communication problems, but also daunting piles of computer print out, imposing reference books and innumerable telexes with advice or instructions from 'head office'. Although it may well be unrealistic to expect them to be able "to take over in 18 months" in all respects, at least progress in the right direction will have been made and good foundations laid for continuing development.

4. The development of human resources is in the long run going to be far more significant to a nation's overall development than any amount of capital projects. Apparently intracticable problems of poverty and disease can be tackled, the natural forces that in the past caused disaster can be controlled and even harnesssed to good effect, the unjust structures can be changed - if the people so mind and they bring the right resources to bear. The least we can do, from our positions of plenty and privilege, is to help give the people of the developing world the tools of knowledge and skills which will enable them to solve, slowly but surely, their own problems and thus build the sort of society they want. The potential is there - it needs to be realised.

5. Training and technology transfer has then to be viewed with a long-term perspective, with continuous development towards the goal of substantial self-sufficiency. Training of course must never stop, since there is always more to learn and young engineers to be trained, but the professional community as a whole will reach the stage where it is capable of undertaking all the nation's projects, bringing in particular expertise where necessary as any consultant or contractor would in the industrialised world. The shorter term objectives of the training programme over the period of a specific project - the 18 months or so of intensive design or construction activity - have to be appropriately set to suit the circumstances, but whatever else is done, every attempt should be made to establish a sound institutional base for on-going training and career development, without which all the good work will quickly be dissipated.

Training needs analysis

6. Training is more an art than a science. There are teaching techniques of course and we all know a good teacher when we meet one, but essentially the development of human resources calls for sensitive planning to provide appropriate opportunities for technology transfer to happen almost imperceptively, if not without effort, at least without too much stress arising in either the giver or receiver. Everyone is willing to acknowledge the importance of training in

general but few like to be labelled "Trainees", with the
implication that they are deficient in various ill-defined
respects.

7.   The need for a thorough training needs analysis should
not be overlooked, since the training objectives and overall
strategy need to be well founded on the real situation, not on
a superficial analysis based on unrepresentative reports.   The
training needs analysis would normally be undertaken by an
expatriate training specialist supported by experienced senior
staff from a local consulting firm, with three main
objectives:

i)   Identification of trainees
        - by organisation
        - by grade (junior, middle, senior, top management)
        - by size of each group

ii)   Identification of requirements and priorities
        - by topic (ie, specific areas of knowledge and skills)
        - by target group

iii)   Identification of an appropriate strategy
        - long-term objectives
        - institutional base
        - short-term programme and budget
        - training staff

8.   Allowing time for adequate consultation and reporting,
at least 6 weeks should be allowed for the necessary training
needs analysis.   The report, when agreed and finalised, will
provide a valuable reference document, setting out the present
status, the long-term objectives and the proposed route to
achieve them.   The proposals must take full account of the
Client's existing training arrangements and institutional
constraints, to ensure the maximum degree of pragmatic fit -
there is no value in proposing arrangements that simply will
not work, however sensible they may appear to an outsider.
This is undoubtedly an area where local advice is essential.

The training programme
9.   Every case is different in detail, but it is likely that
a well-balanced training programme will consist of most if not
all of the following elements:

- On-the-job training
- Individual lectures by specialists
- Tutorials and personal supervision
- Workshops and seminars
- Short training courses (1 - 3 weeks)
- Post-graduate courses (6 months - 2 years)
- Overseas training (short and long courses)

10. Careful attention would need to be given to selecting appropriate methods for the various target groups. Top management would be unlikely to be free for more than one or two days at a time, whereas middle and junior grades could probably be spared for short training courses lasting up to 3 weeks. A few particularly promising candidates would be selected for overseas training, but the main effort would probably be directed to on-the-job training for a group of middle grades, that is those with 4 to 10 years experience since graduation.

11. Training programmes like everything else have to be subjected to budget constraints. The concern will be to find the most cost-effective solutions for situations where the needs greatly exceed available resources. As a rule-of-thumb, it is suggested that a training budget of between 15-25% of the cost of the engineering services required for a project (from both the consulting engineer and the contractor) should be allocated to training, with about 40-50% of that going to on-the-job training.

ON-THE-JOB TRAINING
Target group and methods
12. Wherever practicable, most of the engineering work for overseas projects is these days required to be carried out in the developing country concerned, to facilitate the full participation of local firms and staff from the Client's own organisation, who are generally referred to as counterparts. On-the-job (OTJ) training has to be given to the counterparts as the work proceeds and calls for careful organisation if it is to be effective.

13. The principal methods that are involved in OTJ training include:

- participation alongside the consultant's (or contractor's) expatriate and local staff in all project activities
- explanation of objectives and methods of approach being employed
- regular briefings of individuals and of groups on progress, problems and plans as project work proceeds
- occasional talks and lectures by members of the project team
- personal supervision of individuals, including discussion of preferences, experience, interests, tasks assigned, with progress monitoring.

14. If a significant proportion of the engineering work is to be carried out in the consultants' or contractor's home office, then it may be practicable for several counterparts to be sent there for several months for OTJ and other training activities. Although most of the responsibility for OTJ training is likely to lie with the consultants, it is not uncommon for the contractors engaged for the construction and

for the supply of equipment to be required to take into their organisations counterpart staff for OTJ training.

15. Problems sometimes arise because the counterparts appointed by the client to work with the consultant or the contractor are perceived as being inadequately qualified or committed. No doubt the client does his best to send appropriate people, but he also has to work within constraints and often has little choice himself. Maybe the counterparts do lack experience and/or are not well-motivated, but these are facts to be recognised and accommodated in the training programme. They should never be allowed to become a cause for complaint - training must start from where people are, not where they should be.

Training records

16. A personal training file, similar to the Training Record required by the Institution of Civil Engineers for graduates under agreement, can prove a helpful way to plan and monitor an individual's training. We have evolved a four part record for use on one major project which would seem to have general applicability:

- Part One   Personal Profile
  This part gives personal details of education and experience, and lists areas of strength and weakness in his professional field, plus a summary of personal plans and interests.

- Part Two   Training Objectives
  Taking into account the need to build up a balanced team of counterparts, this part gives recommendations for training objectives in the long term and short term for the individual, with general and more specialised training elements.

- Part Three   Training Programme
  This section outlines the main features of the individual's training proposed for the full period of the project-related training programme, including OTJ training topics, lectures and courses to be attended, recommended reading, field visits and overseas courses, if applicable.

- Part Four   Progress Reports
  At approximately four to six week intervals, the individual and his training supervisor jointly prepare a progress report, listing all the training activities experienced in the period with comments on performance and progress in relation to the original objectives and programme, plus suggestions for future actions to correct any deficiencies.

17. There is no doubt that a personal training record along the above lines provides a useful framework for structuring and monitoring an individual's development. After the initial

effort has been made to complete the first three parts, the regular progress report for Part Four need not present a bureaucratic burden but on the contrary can help the individual feel he is significant and the consultant demonstrate to the client that he is fulfilling his obligations.

Organisation of OTJ training

18. Unless regular procedures are introduced for planning and implementing OTJ training, nothing will happen. This ultimately has to be the responsibility of the project manager, since only he has the knowledge of the various project-related activities that are in progress and the staff members concerned. Counterparts need to be attached to individual members of the consultant's team and appropriate tasks identified, taking into account personalities, experience, skills and interests. This can prove a difficult and sensitive matter, especially when the project manager and his team are under pressure to meet deadlines. The project manager needs advice from his training advisers and senior staff from the local consulting firm to enable him to plan who does what with whom and when.

19. Depending on the nature of the project and the timescale, it is likely that this advice can best be provided at a weekly or fortnightly planning meeting at which OTJ training tasks and appropriate counterparts to work on them can be discussed by the consultant's project team. Unless this is done, there is a real risk that OTJ training will go by default, with counterparts given either too many routine chores or nothing to do at all, which understandably will result in discontent in the ranks.

20. The more the counterparts can be helped to feel that they have a valuable contribution to make to the project, that they can actually help the consultant (or contractor) do his job, the more successful the whole training effort is likely to be. Wherever possible, the regular briefing meetings should be attended by all engaged on the project, not just the counterparts, so that a feeling of involvement is fostered. The attitude adopted by the project manager can make all the difference between OTJ training which is seen as a drag and OTJ training which is seen as a great opportunity to lighten the load at no extra cost.

TRAINING COURSES
Short courses

21. Formal training courses from one to three weeks in duration have a valuable role in under-pinning the OTJ training effort and broadening the base of professionals being trained. The number of counterparts that can be accommodated on OTJ training is limited but formal courses enable many others to be drawn in and introduced to the knowledge and skills being applied in the project. Participants should if

possible be drawn from both public and private sector organisations.

22. The topics for the courses, the target groups, the qualifying conditions, the duration and all the many other details need to be planned to suit the circumstances revealed by the training needs analysis. In most projects, it will probably prove helpful to present an Introductory Training Course as soon as possible after the start, to give everyone concerned (consultant's as well as client's staff) a good orientation with respect to the objectives of the project, the methods of approach, the special techniques likely to be used, policy issues that will need to be addressed, and so on. Micro- computers can be used to good effect in such a course, to illustrate various techniques and provide basic instruction.

23. It is most important that local specialists, drawn from associated consultants, the client's organisation, universities and government departments, are involved to the maximum extent compatible with the objectives of the training course. Their involvement not only brings the benefit of their local knowledge and professional skills but also helps build up an on-going training capability. On a practical level, local lecturers help balance the contributions by relatively few expatriates who would otherwise have a heavy lecturing burden.

24. The training course programme needs to be varied to hold interest and present as many facets of the subject as possible. Group and individual project work, structured discussions, films and field trips can all be worked in with straight lectures as appropriate. Refreshment breaks and meals are also important parts of the programme, providing opportunities for informal contact between the participants and training staff.

Documentation
25. The preparation of appropriate training documentation is of great importance for the success of any training programme. The various types of documentation required include:

- course and lecture notes
- audio-visual aids
- project-related assignments
- sector-related books, reports and papers
- evaluation reports and questionnaires.

26. Experience has shown that the preparation of good documentation requires about three to five man-days for each day of training course. This degree of effort is needed if efficient and effective documentation is to be provided. Lecture notes that summarise the main points are far more useful than verbatim text. The contract should provide for

local lecturers to re-use the documentation when presenting
refresher courses in the same topics.

27. Self-instruction videos are becoming available for
certain topics, particularly for micro-computer programmed
learning. It is the author's view that a low-cost video film
of the training course when first given live would prove to be
a useful aid for consolidation and refresher training, and
considerably cheaper than the cost of bringing back expatriate
specialists for repeat courses.

Overseas training courses

28. In addition to any OTJ training in the consultant's (or
contractor's) home office, a number of overseas training
options may be considered, such as:
- one year university courses leading to a master's degree
- shorter courses (4 - 12 weeks) at universities or training
  institutions
- participation in international conferences and workshops
- study tours, involving brief periods at a number of
  organisations

Careful evaluation of the possibilities and potential
participants is essential. As the costs of overseas training
are very high, relatively few will be able to benefit and
there is a real risk that those that do will in time be lost
to their parent organisations. An overseas qualification may
well prove to be a passport to an overseas job and is highly
sought after for this reason.

29. Although the main emphasis should be directed towards
training a wider group in the country concerned, there is
often a good case for sending a few suitable individuals on
selected overseas courses, particularly if available within
the same geographical region where most of the participants
will come from countries facing similar problems in similar
cultural contexts. Here again the advice of senior staff from
a local firm is needed, to ensure that requests (and there are
sure to be many) for overseas training from the client's
personnel are appropriately dealt with, without too much
disappointment.

TRAINING STAFF
Resident Training Advisers

30. The appointment of a full-time resident training
adviser, if funds allow, considerably strengthens the overall
training programme, as it ensures the presence on the
consultant's (or contractor's) team of someone whose sole
responsibility is to the trainees and who is not therefore
distracted by the inevitable stresses and strains of the main
project. He needs to be someone with good general knowledge
of the subjects being addressed by the main project, a
competent manager and, above all, good with people. Ideally,

he should be assisted by a local training adviser, someone who is respected by the counterparts and who can advise on the local ways of doing things and the standards that may be expected. Moreover, he will be able to communicate with the participants in their own language. A retired senior university lecturer may have just the right qualities.

31. The duties of the training advisers include such matters as:
- regular liaison with the Project Manager and his team
- build up personal relationships with the counterparts, to ensure that they gain maximum advantage from the training programme
- assist in the organisation and implementation of OTJ training
- carry out all detailed planning for the training programme of lectures, seminars, workshops and training courses
- give group and/or individual tutorials on selected subjects to extend and reinforce the training given through lectures and training courses
- monitor performance and progress of individuals and keep detailed records.

In summary, the training advisers present the project to the counterparts and the counterparts to the project. Without their services, there is a real danger that the training efforts will prove unsatisfactory since the project team will find that they lack the time to follow up individuals or organise properly the forthcoming training events.

Lecturers
32. A good engineer is expected to be a good communicator of his ideas, mainly in writing but also when the occasion requires, in oral presentation. Although many claim to have little or no teaching experience, in the author's experience most competent engineers can give (when suitably encouraged!) a competent training lecture. There is undoubtedly much to be gained by involving the project team directly in the training programme and not turn to 'professional' lecturers, who lack the detailed knowledge of the real problems being tackled on the project. A series of lectures for a training course may however come better from a professional lecturer.

33. For those unused to lecturing to an overseas audience, some tactful advice would probably be needed, mentioning points such as:

- speak clearly and not too fast
- make maximum use of the overhead projector to list all headings and main points
- prepare a handout giving in note form all the main points and if possible distribute this a day or so in advance
- make a list of references for further reading

111

- remember the level of the audience: don't speak above their heads or speak down to them
- use local examples where possible to illustrate your points.

34. As previously mentioned, full advantage should be taken of local specialists in all aspects of the training programme. Their contribution is valuable in its own right and also lays the foundation for the ongoing training programme after the project itself has finished. Local univiersities need to be kept informed, so that they can update their own courses in appropriate instances.

CONCLUSION

35. Training is the key to appropriate development, in that in due course it gives to the people the power to determine the shape of their own environment. There are no shortcuts and the training programme has to be planned over a long time scale, but individual major projects executed largely by foreign consultants and contractors provide excellant opportunities for project-related, as distinct from academic, training.

36. The first step to achieving effective technology transfer is to do as much of the work as possible in the country concerned, even though this may increase consultancy costs and take longer. Overseas firms can then more readily participate and learn from close involvement and also the client's personnel can work alongside the expatriates and make their own contribution.

37. On-the-job training is potentially the most effective method, but it needs supplementing with lectures, seminars, workshops and training courses, so that the principles and techniques can be systematically presented and applied, from simple examples to the most complex. The engineers working on the project, both expatriates and locals, in general make the best trainers, provided they are suitably guided by experienced training specialists.

38. Without a thorough training needs analysis, the training programme will lack direction. The overall objectives and strategy need to be clearly established, so that a good institutional base can be built up that will sustain the training effort after the project has finished. Without this institutional base, no amount of training effort, however well intentioned, is likely to succeed. With such a base however, the rewards are truly enormous, for the benefit of all concerned.

39. With good will and good planning, and with the help of local firms who know the local circumstances so much better than the expatriates, both the quantity and the quality of the training given through development aid can be significantly increased. The scope is virtually unlimited and the rewards

are great, not just in generating new business for western consultants and contractors, but also because of the good returns made possible by the investment in human resources.

40. To illustrate many of the points made in this paper, the main features of the training programmes associated with two projects with which the author has been personally associated are given in the Appendix. The author would like to thank his colleagues in Sir William Halcrow & Partners and the other firms associated with those projects for their advice in developing the training programmes and for their participation in the implementation.

APPENDIX - EXAMPLES OF TRAINING PROGRAMMES
Dominican Republic Solar Development Project (IADB funded)
41. The main training elements of this 3 year project being undertaken by Sir William Halcrow & Partners in association with Intermediate Technology Power Ltd are as follows:-

- 6 week Introductory Training Course (all in Spanish) for 17 participants covering the principles and techniques of solar energy conversion, with practical projects
- Two study tours to see solar research centres and demonstration plants, one to USA, Mexico and Puerto Rico and the other to Spain and France
- A series of 8 pilot plants, each designed, built and tested by Dominican engineers with the advice and assistance of the consultants
- The services of an expatriate resident engineer for 20 months, supplemented by visiting specialists

42. By the end of the project, in May 1985, it is envisaged that there will be an effective team of 8-10 Dominican engineers established at the Instituto Dominicano de Tecnologia Industrial (INDOTEC) who will be generally able to sustain themselves, train new entrants and promote appropriate applications for solar energy in their country.

Bangladesh Energy Planning Project (ADB/UNDP funded)
43. The main training elements in this 19 month project being undertaken by a joint venture of Sir William Halcrow & Partners (leader), Motor Columbus Consulting Engineers Inc (Switzerland) and Petroconsultants SA (Switzerland), in association with two local firms, Prokaushali Sangsad Ltd and Technological Services Ltd, are as follows:

- 3 week Introductory Training Course for 25 participants, covering the principles and techniques of energy planning
- On-the-job training for 8 counterpart staff working alongside the consultant's team in Bangladesh
- Short training courses (1 to 3 weeks each) on computer programming, use of micro-computers, energy planning models, energy economics, expansion planning and rural energy issues

- A lecture or talk each week on average, given by one of the
  Consultant's specialists, supplemented by tutorials
- The services of a resident training adviser for 6 months,
  assisted part-time by a local training adviser
- A limited amount of overseas training for selected
  individuals, covering inter alia computer system management
  and maintenance and power system expansion planning.

44. By the end of the project, in March 1985, it is
envisaged that a longer term institutional support project
will have started, funded by the UNDP, through which further
training will be provided as required. A national energy
planning capability is emerging, with institutional base in
the Planning Commission of the Government of Bangladesh and
staffed by a multi-disciplinary team of engineers, economists
and other professionals.

10 The changing role of Consultants

A. R. PARISH, W. S. Atkins Group Consultants, Epsom

SYNOPSIS.   For many years there has been a well understood role for consultants in which design work was undertaken in the home office while a small site staff was responsible for supervision of construction.   This conventional arrangement has continued longer then might otherwise have been expected in overseas projects because of the distribution of oil revenues, however change is inevitable.

INTRODUCTION

1.   British   consultants   have   played   a   leading   role in   the   execution   of   major   international   projects   during this century.   During this time the market for consultancy services   has   shifted   from   being   a   virtually   protected market   servicing   British   overseas   possessions   to   one where   there   is   intense   competition   from   not   only   other international   consultants   but   also   from   local   practices. The   important   international   financial   role   that   the   City of   London   played   during   this   period   has   also   diminished with the capital markets in New York and   Tokyo   providing alternative   sources   of   capital   for   the   international project.

2.   The   underlying   trend   for   more   and   more   civil   and structural   design   work   to   be   undertaken   in   the   client country   has   been   arrested   on   a   number   of   occasions,   the most noticeable of which was the post oil price increase construction   boom   in   the   mid   1970's.   These   perturbations have only delayed and not reversed the trend.

3.   However   British   consultants   have   responded   to   this challenge   in   a   number   of   ways;   by   providing   a   wider   range of   engineering   and   management   services,   providing   higher technology   services,   by   working   with   local   consultants, and   by   working   with   contractors   in   undertaking   turnkey projects.

4.   The   basic   shift   in   the   technician   level   work   to the   developing   countries   is   reflected   in   the   industrial sector where increasingly the output from basic industries is   provided   by   the   developing   countries,   and   developed nations   are   concentrating   upon   the   provision   of   advanced technology products.

Management of international construction projects. Thomas Telford Ltd, London, 1984.

5. The future role for British consultants overseas will often involve collaboration with local consultants on a joint working basis. It is also likely that the turnkey project will find increasing favour in the developing world and the consultants ability to work together with the financial institutions and contractors will undoubtedly result in new opportunities in the future.

THE CONSULTANTS HISTORICAL ROLE
To the mid 1960's
6. In the period prior to World War I British contractors very successfully roamed the world undertaking projects in, for example, Latin America. The opportunities were extensive and Britain was able to capitalise on its considerable engineering experience and abilities in areas where there was no indigenous competition. Other developed countries were also able to benefit from their own industrial background and undertook construction projects in their own geographic areas of influence. To a large extent these trading boundaries were respected and not crossed. Britain was therefore able to enjoy a comfortable position in working in a non-competitive overseas market. American companies at this time were fully committed to expanding the industrial and infrastructural base of the United States and it was to be many decades before their influence was felt.
7. World War I played a considerable role in effecting international change and the old orders that had existed were to alter in the period following the war.
8. At about this time Britain began to relinquish its position of the dominant financial power in the world and this brought about a corresponding contraction in its sphere of influence. It might be an overstatement but in general Britain retreated into serving a home market which included not just the UK itself but the many colonial possessions in Africa and the Indian sub-continent, together with the independent dominions excluding Canada. This was a massive single trading bloc looking to Sterling as the international trading currency and largely protected from imports from other countries.
9. In those circumstances British suppliers, contractors and consultants did not really need to look outside this extensive home market and when they did they found only marginal extra business.
10. This comfortable situation continued after India and various of the colonies became independent states, not so much because of financial ties but as a result of convenience and habit. Engineering standards had been established, and even local codes produced based upon British practices dictated the need to continue to buy British. Other reasons also played their part in the continuing relationship between Britain and its ex-colonies, these included the higher education in Britain

of many of the nationals who were to take up responsible and influential posts in their home countries. The role that British contractors and consultants played was manifested in other areas such as procurement services undertaken by the Crown Agents, and financial, insurance and shipping services provided by the City of London.

11. The period to the mid 1960's saw a still substantial market, albeit in decline as those nations previously dependent upon Britain began to increase their local engineering capability. This move was assisted by the establishment of overseas branches of British companies who were able to provide some of the engineering requirements locally. Overall the effect of operating in this fairly comfortable market was to create a general feeling of complacency amongst British suppliers; a situation that was to have considerable consequences in the decades that followed.

From the mid 1960's to 1973

12. During this period the newly independent commonwealth countries began to benefit from the increase in international trade and raw material prices and started to flex their economic muscles. Britain no longer found itself as the sole or preferential supplier of goods and services; it faced competition in what it had long regarded as its extended home market. With the consequential loss of business in these hitherto protected territories, British companies had perforce to look elsewhere to provide the volume of business to which they were used. The long years of conducting business in the protected home market was now felt, and for the first time in many years they had to compete in the wider world market and many were ill equipped to do so.

13. However this was a period of relative economic optimism and prosperity and many countries, both third world and developed, were engaged in projects to develop their industry and infrastructure. However, in the case of third world countries there had not been sufficient time since their independence for the secondary and tertiary educational programmes to produce the technicians and graduates, much less for the latter to have acquired any great measure of experience. These countries were unable to provide the trained and experienced manpower to fulfill their national aspirations and this lack of manpower was filled very successfully by British consultants.

14. The needs of the client countries and of the consultants reasonably coincided. For the consultants there was the possibility of continuing the method of working to which they were accustomed, with design work undertaken in the home office in the UK and with a small supervision team working at the overseas site. For the client countries it had the advantage, in the circumstances existing, of minimising costs. This situation would

117

likely have continued with a gradual transfer of design responsibility to the client's country as their educational standards and experience increased. It was a relatively comfortable arrangement which substantially ended in 1973.

Post 1973

15. The rapid increase in oil and gas prices in 1973, and continuing subsequently, had a dramatic effect in changing the balance of wealth in the world. The OPEC countries and other oil and gas but non-OPEC countries suddenly became rich beyond anything they could previously have imagined. The developed countries became correspondingly poorer but they established an effective mechanism for re-cycling the excess funds generated from the oil producing nations. The under developed nations became very much worse off as their energy import costs consumed an ever increasing proportion of their GNP.

16. The well known consequence of this shift of wealth was an upsurge of projects, some of considerable economic and social benefit and some less so, in the newly rich countries. However a number of these countries, for example Libya, Saudi Arabia and the Gulf States, have relatively small indigenous populations compared to the scale of the projects they intended to undertake and just did not have the available manpower to meet either technical or non-technical requirements. This lack was made good by major importation of the skills of consultants and managing contractors and by labour from Pakistan, Korea and the Philippines. Even in those countries with substantial populations, Mexico, Venezuela and Nigeria being examples, there was still a need to import those skills that were necessary for projects of a different type or scale from what had previously been attempted.

17. The result was to present a significant opportunity to international consultants not only to obtain major commissions but to preserve for a time a method of working which, as will be discussed in the next section, was becoming obsolescent in the rest of the world. The oil crisis had the effect of obscuring a change, probably an inevitable change, in the way UK consultants handle overseas work.

THE PICTURE TODAY

18. Over much of the developing world which provides a major part of the overseas work of consultants, a great emphasis has been applied over the past 15 or more years to education. The consequence, particularly in countries whose populations contain a high proportion of young people, is an upsurge in the numbers of those who have completed secondary or tertiary education. In the engineering field the result is that substantial numbers are seeking work at technician or engineer level. Governments

118

requiring, through legal sanctions or influence, that a significant part of engineering work should be undertaken by their own nationals. The move began in populous countries such as Mexico and Venezuela but is now spreading elsewhere and applies for example in Saudi Arabia. The consequence is a major move away from conventional consultancy with design carried out in the home office and only construction supervision undertaken in the country of the project. It is a move which is not only promoted by the countries concerned but receives major support from the World Bank as part of its effort for the transfer of technology and the strengthening of indigenous technical resources. It has been recognised that the simple solution of moving a section of the design office from the home country to the project country is not an economical answer, quite apart from not meeting the national aspirations of the host country. In parts of Latin America the cost of an expatriate engineer could readily be three times the cost of a national engineer with similar qualifications and experience, in China the ratio may be over twenty. But such cost is not the only factor since the expatriate will want a significant part of his remuneration in transferable currency which is a drain on an almost always scarce resource. When account is taken of the shadow cost of this foreign exchange, the ratio quoted above becomes even higher.

19. It is also well to record a change which has taken place in what at first sight appears to be a conventional consultancy assignment. To be described as a "Design Contractor" instead of a "Consulting Engineer" may only appear to be a matter of words or a peculiarity of translation. It is not. Increasingly overseas clients are seeing the consultant as another form of contractor who provides design services in accordance with a contract. No longer can the consultant under such arrangements do what he thinks best in the client's interest - the contract rules! This is a major and very unwelcome development which time may well show not to have been in the best interests of the client.

20. Whilst we have seen, and shall continue to see in an increasing number of projects, that the whole or a large proportion of the engineering design of overseas projects will be undertaken by local consultants, there are new trends which will ensure the continuing involvement of responsive British consultants. Many overseas projects have become of such size, complexity, and cost that the traditional role of the consultant is no longer sufficient to guarantee the successful completion. The mobilisation of finance, engineering, construction and training has necessitated the formation of project teams which can bring together for a single project these resources. These total project capabilities are not available in developing countries and British consultants are well

119

placed to take advantage of these new opportunities. Furthermore many complex industrial projects require both output guarantees and consequent operator training which encourages the turnkey project concept. Additionally major projects requiring large sums of capital, particularly in convertible currency, can not be funded entirely by the multi-lateral financial institutions such as the World Bank. Consequently bi-lateral aid plays a substantial part in project finance and the governments providing that aid typically restrict the use of convertible currency to procurement in their own country except, in some cases, a relatively minor amount. Major projects for power generation or industry are attractive to the donors of soft finance, including aid, as a means of providing employment in their national industry. For this reason turnkey projects are of particular interest for the provision of soft loans.

21. Recognising that a large amount of capital which became available to the oil producing countries in the 1970's produced a perturbation in an identifiable trend, it appears that for the future consultants will have three major opportunities in the international market:

Specialist Services
Joint Working
Turnkey projects

THE FUTURE FOR CONSULTANCY
Specialist Services

22. Special skills and the corresponding specialist services are likely to continue to be in demand where they are demonstrably in the forefront of technology. For example the application of advanced computational techniques for the analysis of complex structural problems associated with aseismic design, heat transfer and wind loading. These specialist services are often outside the range of skills available in countries with newly emerging consultancy organisations. Such skills may make possible the project which would otherwise be impractical or make an uncertain project more secure. Compared with the cost of the project and the risk of failure the cost of the best specialist advice is small and it is even small compared with the cost of the engineering and management of the project.

23. This aspect of consultancy services is the counterpart of the general argument that Britain has to move up-market technically if it is to continue to find a demand for its goods and services in a world where more and more countries are producing what were, yesterday, British products. Simple road and drainage schemes are within the capability of most countries and the range is extended in some cases, or will in others, to cover more of the spectrum of civil and structural engineering. While it is not yet the case, it is certainly arguable

that only for technically difficult problems or complex projects will many countries require to import civil and structural engineering skills. The provision of specialist technical and managerial skills is familiar to the British consultant and specialist practices and the specialist sections of the larger wide ranging practices, may well see a strong demand for the services of technologists, but a reduced overseas demand for the services of technicians.

24. The trend towards a reduced technician content does not necessarily imply that consultants will not undertake the basic design and drafting on future projects. By the application of computer aided design and engineering it may be possible to provide a competitive service to that provided by consultants in the developing countries. In addition these systems have the facility for rapidly accommodating design changes which are so often a feature of the complex or "fast tracking" project. This feature may well provide the cost advantage that is needed to compete with the low rates of the emergent consulting engineers in the developing world. Future developments linking together the design-analysis-drafting functions into a single system using a common data base could well give further advantages to the established consultant. However it can only be a matter of time before these techniques are available to all consultants. It is indeed the advent of powerful low cost distributed computing facilities which may well allow the emerging consultant to "leap frog" to a position where they can provide a similar design service currently available from British consultants.

Joint Working

25. In many overseas countries either as a result of special legislation or because of other influences, the foreign consultant acting on his own is not chosen to undertake projects. Even where the foreign consultant is free to operate on his own, shortages of foreign exchange and the consequent restrictions on the remittance of convertible currency result in the need to undertake a significant amount of the work in the project country. The local requirement may be for a jointly owned practice, for a joint venture with a local consultant or for the provision of specialist staff to form a joint team with the client's staff. Whatever may be the cause or the form of the association the effects on the consultant and on his staff are similar.

26. There is no gainsaying the fact that any joint operation in another country produces more problems than a conventional consultancy assignment. The British practice inevitably surrenders some of its freedom of action and while maintaining a professional and local responsibility, some of the ability to control the work and the results.

Detailed joint venture or similar agreements may give a degree of comfort and security, but in the ultimate the basic requirement is confidence between the parties and that in its turn depends upon the relationship between people. The principals of the British practice have a major role in setting the framework for the collaboration, but much of the success depends on the consultants staff who are resident in the project country and working alongside nationals of that country.

27. It is, of course, essential that such staff should be competent in their profession, but in these circumstances personal qualities which are of lesser importance in the home office become profoundly significant. Some of the requirements are:

* Sensitivity to cultural difficulties leading to quite different basic attitudes of the two nationalities.

* Sensitivity to national pride and national aspirations.

* Tolerance of local customs and of the local bureaucracy.

* Recognition that technology transfer is regarded as important and having the corresponding patience to explain and instruct.

* Recognition that senior officials of the host country may be surprisingly young for the responsibility they carry but are nevertheless entitled to respect.

28. Perhaps the cardinal thought for expatriates should be that they are guests in the host country and that it is for them to take the initiative in avoiding or solving problems. A genuine interest in the country, its culture and its history provides a significant bridge across any cultural differences.

29. In cold print this looks very daunting but in reality British engineers have succeeded particularly well in establishing these personal relationships which are important for success. The consultants tradition of loyalty to the interests of his client can be a surprise in some overseas countries but once understood is of the greatest value in cementing the relationship on the project.

Turnkey Projects

30. With a number of large scale overseas projects being undertaken on a turnkey basis there is a demand for consulting skills to supplement and support those

of the turnkey contractor. In general the need will arise when the contract has a content which is either outside the normal scope of the contractor's work, or perhaps less frequently, when the contractor needs to expand his capability in a section of the work. The obvious example would be when an independent turnkey project includes civil engineering which has to be under- taken by a national sub-contractor who lacks design capability.

31. There is an impression that working in this way is in some sense contrary to the consultant's ethical principals, but of course that is not the case. He has a clearly identified client, the turnkey contractor, to whom he owes his loyalty, and no one should be under any delusion about that. However, it can be difficult, at least initially, for the consultant's staff to remember that it is not the owner's interest that they have to safeguard, but the interest of the turnkey contractor. Fortunately this is a confusion that does not long persist.

32. Turnkey projects may well represent an increasing proportion of available overseas general civil engineering design as national capability develops to undertake the major proportion of the general run of civil engineering in the overseas country. In the extreme, general civil engineering design could, apart from turnkey opportunities and joint operations become almost confined to the home market.

11

The establishment of subsidiary company operations in Hong Kong and Malaysia

A. DUNCAN, Henry Boot International Ltd, Sheffield

SYNOPSIS. The author draws upon his own experiences and involvement in the establishment of permanent subsidiary company operations in Hong Kong and Malaysia. The widely differing business environments are described together with the highlighting of a number of problems that face the foreign contractor when he first seeks to enter the market. Problems associated with the availability, selection and appointment of staff are touched upon, as are the subjects of labour, plant and equipment, and sub-contractors. The influence of Government in the construction market place is also commented upon. Lastly the author draws attention to the wide differences in market and operating conditions to be met in the various countries of South East Asia.

INTRODUCTION

1. My company, Henry Boot, has a number of subsidiary companies operating successfully in the Far East. These are based in Hong Kong, Malaysia and Singapore. The establishment of them has taken place progressively over seven or eight years, firstly in Hong Kong then into Malaysia, and more recently in Singapore.

2. Our approach to working overseas has perhaps been different to that of most other contractors, and for this reason my paper may serve as a contrast and comparison with others, but none-the-less offering one approach to the winning and execution of major projects. I will draw from our own experiences in establishing an international contracting activity, taking the widely differing business and political climates of Hong Kong and Malaysia by way of contrast.

3. Company Approach. The only one-off civil engineering projects which my company will consider tendering for in a foreign country, in which we are not already established, are railway projects. These, by their nature, tend to be specialist; they tend to require a measurable proportion of export hardware, and they offer work for our railway engineering factories. These factors tend, in our view to offset some of the risks inherent in carrying out a major project in a country of which we have little, if any, previous experience.

4. Having said that, we regard the establishment of a permanent subsidiary company operation in a foreign country as a less risky approach in the long term, and one which enables us

to identify, bid for and win the higher value major projects
which arise from time to time.

HONG KONG
Background
5. Hong Kong provides a unique environment in which to do
business. Its non-elected Government through its policies and
legislation has encouraged a society dedicated to the creation
and pursuit of wealth, coupled with an acceptance of the need
for hard work in achieving such goals. The result is there
for all to see in Hong Kong's record of growth and industrial
development in recent years. Private enterprise and the
entrepreneur can not complain about the dead hand of
Government interfering with their activities.

6. Thus, at face value there is no impediment to a company
setting up shop in Hong Kong. Profits can be freely remitted,
the maximum rate of corporation and personal tax is 17%, and
the business environment is efficient, well ordered and disc-
iplined in the Western manner.

7. The creation of wealth, with its consequent upward
pressure on living standards has, for a long time, stimulated
a need for a continuing development of its infrastructure,
such as land reclamation, highways, drainage, sewage and water
treatment, power generation, railways, and indeed whole new
towns.

8. The majority of this is the responsibility of Government
Departments or Public Authorities, although in many cases they
employ consulting engineers and architects to act on their
behalf. Tender lists for the Public Works Department (by far
the biggest single source of work) tend to be open, without
select lists, whereas other employing authorities tend to be
selective. However, the Public Works Department do have, for
various categories of work, lists of contractors who have prequalified against certain technical and financial criteria for
inclusion in these lists and only listed contractors can tender.
Furthermore getting one's name on select lists for other
clients is difficult without Hong Kong Public Works Department
approved list status. So a "new boy" contractor venturing into
Hong Kong with a view to establishing a permanent presence has
to concentrate on qualifying himself to bid for Public Works
Department work. And here he may have a problem in that the
financial parameters within which he must fit are unrealistic
and totally unflexible. A period of one or two years gaining
approval in the International Contractor category is not uncommon.

9. Where then does the "new boy" start. A first visit to
Hong Kong provides a bewildering and fascinating range of impressions, which may indeed only serve to confuse. One's
first impression is that the construction industry never sleeps

but works instead a 24 hour shift, for at least six days per week. Little effort seems to be put into the control of noise, be it caused by piling hammers, compressors or pneumatic tools. Safety standards are extremely low, (for example, one can often step across bare wires twisted together, lying on a wet pavement as a shop fitter goes about his work).

10. Bamboo scaffolding soars ten or fifteen storeys high above one's head, while suspended floors are carried by modern lightweight steel support systems.

11. Huge multi-storey buildings may be founded on hand-dug caisson piles: a traditional time tested method of large diameter piling, which is essentially sub-let on a pile-by-pile basis to husband and wife teams. He digs, she mans the winch and bucket, and generally watches over husband's head. Again one can see a high output Japanese back-hoe excavator machine working in close proximity to hand excavation using wicker baskets for carrying the spoil, sometimes using women as the labourers.

12. Such contrasts can only serve to confuse or perhaps intimidate the prospective contractor, particularly when such impressions are overlain with such a distinctive Chinese flavour. All construction labour is Hong Kong Chinese, no foreign labour being allowed in to the Territory, with the exception of housemaids from the Philippines.

13. On the other hand, brief investigation reveals an extremely well ordered business environment with excellent banking, legal, telex, telephone and postal services. There is a highly efficient range of support industries be they plant, and equipment suppliers, shipping and forwarding agents, suppliers of goods and services. Indeed virtually anything can be made or obtained in Hong Kong. Contract documents are clearly written, and contract letting procedures, (certainly in the public sector) are strictly adhered to. Commissions and introduction fees do not exist in the public sector, and are rare in the private sector. Thus as a contracting environment, there is a lot of attraction to one used to working in perhaps less well ordered parts of the world.

14. Our own entry into Hong Kong was by way of tendering for a specialist railway tracklaying contract for the first stage of the Hong Kong Mass Transit Railway. The contract called for reinforced concrete plinth foundations. A joint venture agreement was entered into with a large and successful Hong Kong based contractor, both companies in effect being able to offer something to such a joint venture. In this way the local knowledge of our partners was grafted onto our specialised knowledge, and a competitive and ultimately successful bid was the result. The Joint Venture Agreement was restricted to a single contract arrangement.

15. Thoughout the period of the contract our local knowledge developed, as did our understanding of climate and ground conditions. Sub-contractors and suppliers became known to us, and most importantly with this knowledge grew our confidence. We came to realise we were as competent as the Japanese, or French, or local Hong Kong companies.

16. We were after two years or so, actively considering entry into the local arena for general civil engineering work, yet were conscious that in so doing we could be biting the hand of our partners. However, we had by this time, agreed to bid together for the next tracklaying contract for Stage II of the Mass Transit Railway. We have retained this relationship for Stage III and have joined forces again in bidding for the Singapore Mass Rapid Transit.

17. It was clear that in order to bid for the larger civil engineering contracts we had to be registered as an approved international contractor. Local contractors are required to work their way up the league in terms of approved status, starting in the smallest job category where we would clearly not be competitive. Registration took us two years, part of the procedure being reference back to the home country via the Local Diplomatic Post.

Labour
18. In the meantime we had set about training our own labour force, and while this was essentially orientated towards track-laying nevertheless a number of our employees proved adept at learning new skills. We departed from normal Hong Kong pract-ice, developing a core of directly employed permanent labour and supervision, instituting incentive schemes where appro-priate. This appealed to the Chinese enthusiasm for working hard and making money.

19. It is important that you learn as quickly as you can the local custom and practice with regard to employment of labour. The employer is expected to entertain all his employees with dinner (Chinese) and entertainment, preceded by Mah Jong, once or twice a year. Superstition is rife and the employer must always be aware of "Fung Shui" or what can be deemed to be good or bad luck, auspicious or inauspicious. The presentation of Orange Trees and the killing of pigs may also have to be taken into consideration!

20. Another part of our philosophy was to develop as rapidly as we could, a portfolio of labour-only and specialist sub-contractors who we could rely on, and who, as importantly, could rely on us. We tried where possible to stick to comm-itments made, paying promptly and treating fairly. This we believe in the long run enables one to bid more competitively.

Staffing

21. There is no problem in attracting expatriate staff to Hong Kong. The market level of salaries, coupled with the tax level at 17% must make it perhaps one of the most attractive postings in the world. It is fair to say that the after tax rewards to an employee working in a number of other more arduous and unpleasant areas of the world do not bear comparison with his colleagues in Hong Kong, taking all things into account. In fairness, working hours tend to be longer, and the demands of the job can at times be more taxing than in the U.K. A company is governed to some extent by market forces in setting levels of remuneration and fringe benefits, but being market levels they should not affect one's competitiveness, Hong Kong levels remain distorted and are, I believe a legacy of former days. Just as surely, however, market forces will gradually bring local and expatriate terms and conditions close together.

22. Going back in time a thorough appraisal of local living conditions was carried out. Typical flat accommodation was visited and photographed, schools were visited, supermarkets and departmental stores looked at and shopping lists priced. The first team we sent out to Hong Kong were entertained, with wives, to a travel film on the Territory, given a slide show and talk, together with sight of a folder containing photographs of accommodation.

23. We prepared our first in-house staff overseas service Agreement based on an amalgam of what we considered to be the better points of those Agreements in use with other U.K. companies who were most helpful when advice was sought. Over the years we have fine tuned the Agreement, although it remains essentially similar to the original.

24. As far as accommodation was concerned we decided upon a monthly rental limit, together with a lump sum allowance for furnishings, and then allowed the individual or couple to seek and furnish accommodation to their liking. This is perhaps marginally more generous than other approaches to the problem but it does virtually eliminate future complaints and personnel problems arising from discontent among wives.

25. Careful selection of staff is vital. Many articles have been written on the subject but I believe that in the long run gut-feel counts for a lot. Those selecting staff must know the country or territory and must be particularly aware of the relevant national characteristics and sensitivities, as well as the probable life style imposed on the individual and his family. Though there are alternatives, generally speaking, living in Hong Kong requires a family to accept high rise living with no garden. Public transport is very limited. Sophisticated entertainment, bars, discos, and restaurants abound. On the other hand, sports and recreational activities are in short

supply and very expensive. For this reason the company in-
vested in a motorised leisure junk, which is available to all
staff and their families. The sea and surrounding islands
provide perhaps the most relaxing way of getting away from
high rise living and the densely packed city which is Hong Kong.

Legal and Taxation Aspects

26. Our initial entry into Honk Kong was, as I described earlier, as a member of a joint venture. The concept of a joint
venture as such was new to us, and we made the mistake of not
properly researching the legal and tax aspects of our status in
Hong Kong. As a result through insufficient thought being applied to these matters at a very early stage, we were not able
to structure our accounts to take best advantage of the tax
rules in Hong Kong and the U.K. It was a lesson we fortunately
learned early-on in our international history. But time spent
in consultation with local professional advisers prior to
taking irrevocable steps in the drawing up of joint venture
agreements, and the setting up of subsidiary companies is time
well spent. Indeed it may be necessary to decide upon the right
company vehicle for a particular project one or two years in
advance of the ultimate tender date. Once one has registered
initial interest in a particular project with a client, it can
be very difficult persuading him that you wish to change your
nominated subsidiary company to a different one.

Business Development

27. Some four years after our entry into Hong Kong we were
approached by a very reputable private landscaping company,
based in the U.K. but with Middle East experience, with a
view to setting up a joint company to seek business in what
was identified as a rapidly growing market. After the appropriate research was carried out, a new company Henry Boot
Clapham was formed in Hong Kong. Land was found (not without
difficulty) and an agreement reached to rent from no less than
twelve separate landowners, in order to develop a nursery for
trees and shrubs. It is fair to say that an entrepreneurial
attitude quickly develops in Hong Kong. I would doubt if our
approach to such a proposition would have been necessarily the
same elsewhere in the world. I am pleased to say that the
company has gone from strength to strength and can now be
regarded as perhaps the premier company of its type. In this
case we married our own local knowledge, contacts and contractual experience to a sound "green-fingered" family business,
with satisfying results to both sides.

Subsequent Joint Ventures

28. In the last three years or so my company has, in Hong
Kong, participated in a number of joint venture bids and
consortia, generally with local companies. The general yardstick for two companies to associate together in such a way is
as it is for anywhere else, namely a sharing of risk and a
combination of strengths to mutual benefit. There does seem a

flexibility of attitude there which permits an easier association of rival companies.

Plant and Equipment
29. There is virtually no developed plant hire industry,
while the ready mixed concrete industry is less developed than
in say the U.K. As a result contractors tend to buy and own
most of their plant. Their problem is where to keep it. Land
is in such short supply that one's sites tend to act as temporary plant yards.

Conclusion: Hong Kong
30. I hope that what I have outlined in the first part of my
paper has given you some insight into the Hong Kong construction market. You may ask whether or not recent negotiations
on its future will affect the opportunities for contractors
from outside the "colony". Crystal balls are not part of my
stock in trade, so I will leave that judgement for you to make.

31. I would like now to turn to Malaysia, by way of contrast.

MALAYSIA
Background
32. Malaysia is a rapidly developing independent nation,
consisting of three large land masses: Peninsular Malaysia,
which lies south of Thailand, Sabah and Sarawak. These last
two States form part of the huge island of Borneo. Peninsular
Malaysia is separated from Sabah and Sarawak by several hundred
miles of the South China Sea.

33. The Peninsular is the most developed area of the country,
whereas Sabah, and particulary Sarawak, are only now embarking
on any measurable degree of development.

34. The source of Malaysia's wealth of course used to be founded on tin and rubber, but in more recent years, a broader based
economy has emerged; oil, gas, timber, palm oil, pepper, the new
crop of cocoa, and lastly manufactured goods are all vital elements in her G.N.P.

35. In looking at the prospects for an international contractor in Malaysia it is necessary for one to be aware of the
political and social climate in the country. There are three
main ethnic groups; the Malays or "bumiputras" (which means
"Sons of the soil"), the Chinese, and the Indians. These people
represent approximately 50%, 40% and 8% respectively of the population. The balance of 2% are represented by other minority
nationalities.

36. Historically, the industrial and commercial wealth of the
country was concentrated on the Western side of the Peninsular,
and rested largely in the hands of Malay Chinese. In recent
years, the Malay bumiputras, who hold political power, have em-

barked on a programme of "social engineering", whereby through
fiscal and other incentives and legislation the encouragement
and development of bumiputra business and commerce has been
fostered.

37. The phrase "technology transfer" frequently occurs in
Government prenouncements as being something that should be
built into any licensing arrangement, joint venture, shareholding or other business agreement. Government contracts
again will frequently include a requirement for training of
Malays within the framework of the contract: or where a substantial amount of imported hardware is involved, a long term
commitment to build a manufacturing plant, or at the least an
assembly plant may be called for.

38. The Prime Minister has pronounced a "Look East" policy,
expanding the virtues of the Japanese in their attitude to work
and their business and trading structure, while highlighting
the shortcomings of the Western approach to such things. More
recently however the official view has become more pragmatic,
with the advantages and disadvantages of both systems being more
equally identified.

39. In parallel with the elected system of Government, there
exists the historical system of each State having its Sultan
and Royal Family. There is a King of Malaysia who is elected
by agreement from among the Sultans. The Sultans have little
true political power, but wield considerable power and influence
in their home State, both because of their wealth and their position.

40. As a consequence of this political and ethnic background
it is almost imperative that a foreign contractor cooperates
in some way with a Malaysian company, and for obvious reasons
preferably one with "bumiputra status". This term describes a
company with a bumiputra shareholding above a certain percentage
and with genuine bumiputra involvement at senior management
level. When the declared policy of Government is the encouragement and enhancement of the bumiputras, and with so many of
the decision makers in the Public Sector being bumiputras, the
inference is there to be drawn.

41. The task of course is to find the right partner, one who
can offer the right mix of contacts, experience, advice, integrity and commitment. One can only do this by spending time
and money on the country, getting to know "how it ticks", talking to banks, accountants, architects, engineers etc., and above
all not rushing into a marriage without a reasonable honeymoon
period!

The Malaysian Construction Industry
42. In the course of time, the industry will evolve and settle
down into some semblance of order. At the present time however,

perhaps because construction contracts tend to involve big numbers, a large number of people are attracted into entering the market, usually with little experience or financial substance. Quite large public authority tenders will attract upwards of sixty bidders, with the inevitable result that the lowest bidders will be those companies making mistakes or having inadequate experience. It will take some years for the lessons to be learned, and for the advantages of select lists and the establishment of registers of properly vetted contractors to be recognised. There are contracts for which prequalification is sought but these are the exception rather than the rule.

43. The sub-contractor role is fairly well defined and developed in Malaysia. The majority of these tend to be Chinese owned or managed. A glance at the high standard of building finishes achieved in the impressive developments in Kuala Lumpur will confirm this. However, perhaps inevitably, skilled sub-contractors are less plentiful outside the capital city, where of course most of the development has been. But the situation is changing, particularly as the discovery of oil and gas off the East Coast of Malaysia has prompted large scale development of related process industries, basic heavy industry and infrastructure along the East Coast.

44. There is a considerable amount of earthmoving equipment throughout the country. The reason for this is that there has been considerable development of new rubber and palm oil estates, with a related demand for estate roads. As a consequence, earth moving sub-contract rates are extremely competitive, but many of the quoting companies have little knowledge of working to tight specifications and tolerances. At tender stage their low quotes create problems for an experienced contractor, who owns his own plant and who is seeking a realistic return on his investment.

Our Own Experience

45. In the case of Henry Boot, we first got to know Malaysia through bidding for a 200 kilometre railway reconstruction and refurbishment job, which first came out for tender at the beginning of 1980. We identified a small company run by two elderly expatriates who had both, in earlier years, worked for Malayan Railways, before the country achieved independence. A small sister company had "bumiputra status"; that is, its shareholding reflected a majority held in the hands of bumiputras. A joint venture agreement was entered into, albeit the share of equity was so arranged as to reflect the relative sizes of the two companies.

46. During a prolonged tender, re-tender, and third tender period we entered into an agreement to purchase our joint venture partner company and to purchase a minority interest in its associated bumiputra company.

47. We recognised that doing this would not give us instant

success to the market, but rather an association with a Malay business partner with whom we got on, and who recognised the mutual benefits to be gained from such a relationship.

48. Since the purchase of shares we have contributed a considerable amount of management, time and money into the company, regarding this as an investment for the future. At the time of writing we are in the final negotiations for the award of a £50M contract for the civil works associated with a telecommunications project covering the whole of Malaysia, in association with a German company responsible for the communications equipment. This contract would not have been won without our having put in three years thorough spadework. This has enabled us to understand the politics of Malaysia, and the importance of personal contact. It has also given us the knowledge and experience of working in various remote parts of the country; often a two or three day journey from home base, perhaps employing local tribesmen through the good offices of the headman, and often in security restricted jungle areas. So our initial investment looks likely to give us a return. And we can, I believe, regard ourselves now as firmly established, with a long term outlook for the future.

Labour
49. The ethnic mix does present some managerial problems, but these are largely kept to a minimum by having the right supervisors as foremen; and it is possible to find, and/or develop such people. There are no trade unions to speak of. There is a shortage of skilled craftsmen. As I described earlier however there is a developing sub-contract industry.

Staff
50. For reasons of cost, and because of the difficulty in obtaining work permits, and lastly for reasons of national sensitivities, it is not practical to develop any operation in the country with a large expatriate management team. There are excellent younger qualified engineers available, the product of the explosion in secondary and university education in recent years. There is, however, currently a shortage of experienced, qualified Malaysian middle-managers. This problem will over the years sort itself out, but in the meantime the situation is not easily covered.

51. Living conditions are generally very attractive, particularly in the bigger towns. Good quality accommodation is usually available for rent, there is a good choice of food and other goods in the shops, entertainment is available, and a pleasant relaxed life style can be enjoyed. Sporting facilities are available, and the climate is particularly conducive to swimming.

52. The more remote areas of course, such as Sabah and Sarawak are limited in what can be offered, and long term postings of

single staff are therefore not recommended. Schooling, particularly in Kuala Lumpur is good up to the age of 10 or 11,
after which it can be a problem.

Legal and Tax Aspects

53. The taxation system in Malaysia is not particularly generous, and this part has therefore to be watched in fixing
remuneration levels.

54. Profits can be freely remitted, and the flow of capital
into and out of the country does not generally create a problem.

55. The banks have virtually all been "Malayanised", but this
has not greatly changed anything. A number of well known British Banks have good local connections.

56. The Malaysian legal system is based on the British system.
It is fair to say, however, that it is beginning to creak a
little due to it not having been able to keep abreast of the
demands increasingly thrust upon it as a consequence of Malaysia's rapid growth in recent years.

Plant and Equipment

57. Although not as highly developed as in Hong Kong, nevertheless a good cross-section of plant and equipment manufacturers is represented in Malaysia, with good stocks of spares. The
plant hire industry however is to all intents and purposes non-
existant. Ready Mixed concrete as an industry is in its infancy.

58. Vehicles are in good supply both in delivery and choice.
Restrictions on choice may be made however, when the new Malaysian car appears on the roads.

Conclusion

59. I have found, as we have developed our business activities
in the Far East, that the differences between neighbouring countries or states are much greater than, say between two countries
in Western Europe. Their cultures, political and legal systems,
business methods, geography, and indigenous construction industries are often strikingly different. Thus one can rarely transfer lessons learned but must start again, from scratch. But
with practice, one can learn to compete on an equal footing with
other foreign contractors. I hope my paper has been of interest,
and offers an alternative to the "Project Approach" to working
overseas.

12 The experiences of a medium sized construction company in the Middle East

H. W. TRY and M. A. F. RUSH, W. S. Try Construction Group, Uxbridge

SYNOPSIS. This paper attempts to explain why a medium sized building contractor became interested in the Middle East and describes how the first project was obtained and executed with some observations on this salutary experience.

In 1975 W.S. Try Limited was looking at the prospects in the United Kingdom from the point of view of continuing its profitable growth. The prospects did not look encouraging and it was a time when the siren call of overseas work was sounding most persuasively.

We therefore decided to examine the opportunities in the overseas areas where construction work was most active which, at the time, were Nigeria and the Middle East. We quickly ruled out Nigeria on the basis of the difficulties in taking the monies earned out of the country and we therefore concentrated on the Middle East.

We first spent some months talking to friends in London who had experience in the Middle East. These included architects, engineers, quantity surveyors and a number of friendly contractors. Contractors were very much readier to talk about the prospects and their real experience in the Middle East than they would ever be in talking to a competitor about their work in the United Kingdom. We gained a great number of impressions and a certain amount of hard information. We also built up a list of introductions, some in the United Kingdom but many in the Middle East, principally to the Middle Eastern offices of the firms or practices we had been talking to or to associates and clients of those firms.

We then went off on a fact finding tour taking in, in only three weeks, Saudi Arabia, Dubai, Sharjah, Abu Dhabi, Oman and Qatar. Clearly this could give no more than a superficial impression to add to the information we had already built up, but it was valuable even in that short time in giving a flavour of the local conditions and of the people concerned.

We concluded that Saudi Arabia was the biggest construction market, least well served by international contractors or by local contractors. It was however clearly the most difficult market in which to operate, with the most difficult physical conditions, the least developed infrastructure and with poor back up in terms of hotels, telephones, port facilities, etc.

The other countries we visited were preferable in every respect except that they had well established competition from international contractors, particularly British companies, and a volume of work much smaller than that of Saudi Arabia. We therefore decided that Saudi Arabia represented the best opportunity for a company new to the field in the sense of being the place where we would be least disadvantaged by being a newcomer.

It was clear that a number of large companies had established offices in Saudi Arabia before obtaining any work and some had been there as much as two years incurring very considerable expense with nothing to show for it. We decided that we would endeavour to obtain our first contract from the United Kingdom by contact with U.K. consultants and the opportunity arose through the engineers, Buro Happold, and quantity surveyors, Widnell & Trollope, to tender for the worlds largest enclosed cable net structure - the sports hall of King Abdul Aziz University in Jeddah.

This was a very unusual project and might at first sight appear to be undesirable as a contracting company's first introduction into a new country where the physical conditions and organisational problems were only to be guessed at. On examination however it had many of the most desirable qualities. The superstructure, although unusual, was structurally very simple in concept and was to be supplied and erected very largely by nominated sub-contractors. The project was of about the right size from the bonding and interim finance point of view and our own work in the foundations and floor slab appeared reasonably uncomplicated.

The sports hall was unmistakably Arabian in concept. It was designed by Professor Frei Otto of Buro Gutbrod with Ove Arup & Partners Saudi Arabia and Buro Happold as structural engineers with Brandi Ingenieure as mechanical and electrical consultants and Widnell & Trollope as quantity surveyors. The design team originally produced an imaginative scheme including an adjoining sports village with a forecast cost of £16 million. The budget however was savagely cut by the client to £5 million and with the cuts out went a number of ideas for cladding the tent including the application of stainless steel shingles. Professor Otto calculated that he could still provide the complex if a plastic cladding was acceptable, to which the client agreed. The proposed tent consisted of eight steel masts supporting a cable net, in turn supporting an inner skin of thin plastic fabric and an outer skin of a heavier plastic based material separated by an air gap. This unusual structure to be created in a far away place is reported to have produced few people ready to tender for the specialist superstructure work and in the end the nominated sub-contract for the structure went to a Swiss company,

Habegger, which is better known for the construction of Alpine cable car systems with which there is a considerable similarity in technique. The main contract went out to tender in 1977 and was won by W.S. Try (International) Limited. Work started on the site early in 1978.

W.S. Try were responsible for the construction of the 187 ground anchors, the foundations, and the power floated concrete ground floor slab. When this work was completed eight 800 and 600 millimetre diameter 30 meter high steel masts were lifted into place and temporarily anchored with guy ropes. The cables were then laid out on the ground to a pre-arranged pattern on a half metre grid with special fixings for the external and internal skins arranged at 4 metre intervals.

Habegger had appointed German consultant Ingenieur Planung Leichtbau to study Buro Happold's design and provide a cutting pattern with a 3 millimetre tolerance only for all the cables and they arrived on site as individual lengths varying between 2 metres and 145 metres. A cutting pattern for the plastic fabric covering was also produced by computer.

At each intersection of the cables a clamp was fitted to secure the net together. The complete laying out and the fitting of 57,000 clamps took eight weeks. With the 10,000 metre cable net lying on the ground like a huge fallen spiders web the next step was to set about hauling the net up the masts which took about two days.

The tent was secured to the ground by steel anchorages set into an irregularly shaped 500 millimetre deep reinforced concrete ring beam pinned to the sand with 187 10.5 metre long ground anchors set at 3 metre centres.

The setting out of the ring beam required extremely close tolerances which were somewhat difficult to obtain in the rather adverse conditions of desert working. However they were obtained without serious problems. The ground anchors proved more of a technical problem as one of the best known specialists in the United Kingdom came to the conclusion that the ground would not stand the tensile stresses from the ground anchors. Fortunately soil mechanics and geological considerations are not as exact a science as civil engineers sometimes believe and so a number of other specialists were quite prepared to guarantee that the tensile stresses could be met. Much to our relief we found a very competent British firm who carried out this work and the subsequent tests on the ground anchors showed a more than adequate factor of safety.

The main ridge and stay cables were withheld by large anchorage blocks at ground level each locked into position by a group of seven ground anchors. After the net was anchored to the ring beam the final winching took up all the slack as the net stretched out exactly as planned. Once the pulleys had been removed from the mast head the second stage of the erection could get under way to give the tent its final shape.

Temporary steel beams were fitted through the bottom of each mast to enable the mast to be jacked upwards thereby tightening the net. Working loads were designed to be between 150 and 220 tons depending on the size of the mast with a theoretical lift of about 400 millimetres although these were exceeded slightly to accommodate relaxation. This was a very important part of the operation as it determined which of the wrinkles in the net left after primary lifting were permanent ones - although small inconsistencies were solved by moving grid clamps slightly. It was also an operation whose specific sequence could only be determined as it was under way and one which was temperature dependent. Final pre-stressing had to be done early in the morning when the temperature was about 37° centigrade although the maximum design temperature was 20° centigrade more.

A 1,500 millimetre deep mast base incorporating a sand pot bearing is a detail common on cable net jobs with which Professor Frei Otto has been involved. As the mast is jacked sand is poured through a perforated plate to take up the space created. This acts as a bearing and provides a hinged joint but at Jeddah a rubber pot bearing was also installed to provide the hinge movement following slip circle analysis. The use of sand in the fine adjustment of the masts seemed nicely appropriate to the desert location.

The level of the floor slab to the whole sports complex was something which had to be very carefully considered. We were surprised to realize that in desert conditions although some years pass with virtually no rain, tremendous storms can occur and flash flooding can be a problem. The arrangements for disposing of any flood water in the absence of any storm water drainage facilities and with an underlying impervious layer of rock below the surface were not easily achieved. Our calculations showed that an enormous volume of water could occur from the maximum short term storm possibilities particularly bearing in mind the run off from the two acres of roof surface.

The ground slab of the tent had to be finished to very close tolerances and we adopted a mechanical troweling process. The location of joints, bay sizes to avoid curling, shrinkage and cracking and the protection of the slab from the heat of the sun gave us a number of headaches. In our original considerations we thought it probably best to erect the tent and cast the ground slab afterwards in order to gain the maximum protection and regular conditions for the concreting process. However the delays in the computer detailing of the design and fabrication of the superstructure gave us no choice but to proceed with the slab before the superstructure was in place. In the event this worked extremely successfully and demonstrated what high quality work can be achieved by careful supervision and using relatively unskilled imported labour from the third world.

The cable net supported an outer membrane of a white translucent acrylic coated and panama woven material encased with pvc and finished with acrylic, to reduce ultra violet degradation, provide the required amount of fire resistance, and give an acceptable finish and strength. The inner membrane was supported below the cable net structure on pretzel shaped hangers and was of a lighter more translucent material than the outer membrane. The white outside coat now has a sand covering and most of the tent is a deep yellow/beige colour. Despite the sand staining about 2,000 lux permeates the membranes giving adequate natural lighting for most activities during the day time. Following the erection of the outer membrane work on the project stopped while Phase II, the construction of pre-cast concrete stands, was agreed at a further cost of approximately £2 million.

Work resumed with W.S. Try (International) Limited as main contractor pouring the 12 no. 90 ton reinforced insitu concrete portals inside the tent. The terrace units were pre-cast on the sports hall floor slab and lifted into place. After the structural work was complete the inner membrane of the tent was erected by joining together several fields and winching the completed lining up to the cable net roof.

The two skin membrane of course had the inevitable problem of sand depositing on the inner membrane surface and whereas the wind tended to keep the thickness of deposit on the outer membrane within reasonable limits this did not apply to the inner membrane. The occasional cat climbing on the inner membrane left an interesting pattern of paw marks in the sand on the flatter areas and skid marks on the steeper areas.

The plenum formed between the two membranes was designed to act as a large natural ventilation duct for the tent. All fresh air for the air conditioning system is drawn from this plenum into 14 peripheral air handling units which cool the air and project it into the playing and spectator areas. Hot air is extracted at the top of each mast by means of large centrifugal fans mounted on special platforms. Air is also extracted from beneath each seat on the spectator stands to be exhausted or re-treated for re-circulation as the conditions demand. Relatively cool air from the prevailing south west winds off the Red Sea are used during the winter months for cooling after the fashion of the traditional Bedouin tent. This assists in minimising the cooling load in the summer time.

Completion of the mechanical and electrical installation was carried on in parallel with the high quality finishes to the stands where stainless steel handrails, carpet and over 1,300 cloth upholstered seats were installed. The sports playing area was covered with a Descol seamless multi purpose polyurethane sports floor. This accommodated various services including a variety of courts and playing areas for hockey, tennis, basket and hand ball as well as gymnastics and fencing. Changing cabins located at each end of the

141

stands incorporated a remote control console for the total mechanical and electrical facilities of the building.

The project was completed on time and to the general satisfaction of the consultants and University authorities and the sports hall was officially opened by His Majesty King Khalid in April 1981.

From the experience of setting up this first project in Saudi Arabia and from experience gained on subsequent projects the following factors are particularly relevant to the medium sized contracting organisation.

It is extremely difficult for the smaller organisation to find a heavy weight Saudi sponsor or partner. The most powerful partners can confine themselves to major international companies capable of carrying out a wide range of work types without limit on value. We found that when we, very sensibly in our eyes, attempted to limit the size of project we were prepared to undertake, this instead of being thought of as sensible and readily to be explained, actually made a potential partner most unhappy. He was reluctant to talk about a limitation on his company's ability to take on work but wished to be able to say that his company could tackle anything.

It is difficult for the newcomer to assess the standing in the business community of a potential partner. You cannot call up an Extel card or look at publicly filed accounts and much will depend in any case on his personal standing with his peers. It is even more difficult to weigh up the many "middlemen" both British and Middle Eastern who will descend on the innocent contractor with ardent and conflicting advice.

The whole question of using a Joint Venture Company or operating as an independent foreign company exercised our judgement ending up with our operating in both ways in different situations. As an independent company one has full control of the management and therefore is in the best position to maximise the efficiency and profitability of the operation. However it does have the disadvantages of being somewhat handicapped in dealing with the local petty officials and of course being subject to local taxation as a foreign company.

The alternative of a Joint Venture Company overcomes these difficulties but gives rise to many more problems of involvement in the running of the company. Cultural differences, educational differences and language barriers can breed distrust between staff at various levels and give rise to unwelcome problems which can divert attention from the real issues. Our experience was that it was much more successful to run your own show and face up to the taxation problems rather than have to share the management responsibility. Inevitably in the Joint Venture Company the local partner is always the stronger at the end of the day and even if one completes a number of successful building

contracts the "local factor" may prevent you from
participating in the profits in the manner expected.

We were very interested in the reaction of our U.K.
employees to the establishment of an overseas subsidiary. We
were surprised by the number of first class contracts
managers, surveyors, and site agents who having spent the whole
of their careers in the U.K. were volunteering for a stint in
Saudi Arabia. It was of course an immense advantage to have
competent trust worthy people prepared to staff our first
project. We felt that it was better to have a good
proportion of our own people unfamiliar though they were with
the local conditions, rather than rely entirely on recruiting
people with Middle Eastern experience who were completely
unknown to us.

No doubt the major reason for the enthusiasm for Saudi
Arabia was the rather gloomy prospect for salary increases in
the U.K. at that time and the attraction of a tax free salary
of twice the U.K. income in Saudi Arabia. Nevertheless the
spirit of adventure played some part and involvement overseas
had an interesting beneficial effect on morale in the Group
as a whole.

We found that we had to develop our own Conditions of
Staff Service for operating overseas. We opted for four
months work followed by two weeks leave in the U.K. This at
the time gave shorter working periods than many contractors
who were tending to work on six or even twelve months in
Saudi Arabia before leave entitlement. However we believe the
slightly lower salary scale and better working conditions
gave a more efficient operation. However one does have to
bear in mind that two weeks leave in every four months does
effectively mean that one in eight of your staff are always on
leave and it is necessary to gear up staffing ratios
accordingly. In fact the leave works out to be little more
than staff enjoy in the U.K. but as it is staggered through
the year rather than being concentrated in Public Holiday
periods it does tend to be more disruptive. Surprisingly a
basis of six day working, ten hours per day, never really
caused any adverse reaction as there was little else to do.
It is interesting to note that if one were to calculate the
appropriate U.K. overtime rates for such a long working week,
the contractor is paying very little premium for the overseas
working element. Of course the employee does benefit from
the no tax advantage and the company does have to bear the
considerable cost of accommodation, food, fares and medical
expenses all of which are the employees responsibility in the
U.K.

At our base in Jeddah and subsequently in Riyadh, we
provided a good standard of accommodation with a swimming
pool and other facilities and these were very much
appreciated. It is of course an almost impossible conundrum
to work out the cost/benfit of such expenditure. It is
perhaps typical of the Saudi Arabian scene that whereas many
contracts are on the basis of the temporary camp facilities

put up by the contractor reverting to the employer at the
end of the contract, our particular contract did not contain
such a clause. However, the employer at the University felt
that our facilities on site were so attractive as to demand
that they were handed over at the end of the project, for a
staff club or visiting students. When one is waiting for
outstanding interim payments in a far off foreign country
there is little one can do to stand up to such a demand,
particularly bearing in mind that once the compound is
dismantled the value of re-claimable items is very limited.
However in our experience such a negotiating technique has
to be expected in the Arab world as the norm, rather than the
exception.

The medium sized contractor is unlikely to have
previously encountered the well developed network for the
recruitment of Indian, Pakistani, Thai, Phillipino, etc.
workers into the Middle East. This is arranged through
labour agents who on the whole provide a relatively trouble
free way of finding and bringing together a major labour
force capable of standing up to the climatic conditions.
However, they still have to be welded together into an
effective working unit.

A major consideration for a medium sized company is the
bonding and the financing problem. The Saudi Arabian
monetary authorities place strict limits on which banks may
establish themselves in Saudi Arabia and this means that
major British banks are not represented on the ground in
Saudi Arabia. Facilities can be arranged through a correspond-
ent bank but it may be that an approach to one of the
authorised banks operating in Saudi Arabia will result in a
better understanding of the local conditions. Although very
few performance bonds have been called by the Saudi Arabian
Government they cannot be entered into lightly, and are in
practice extremely difficult to bring to an end. Any attempt
to refuse to extend the validity of a performance bond even
long after the project is completed can be very difficult as
the authorities normally require that either you extend the
bond or they will call it.

During the currency of our first projects we generally
found the timing of interim payments to be rather slow but
not unreasonable. After practical completion however it can
be very difficult to get further payments, and there are
many obstacles of social security certificates and tax
certificates to be overcome before a final payment can be
expected. As oil revenues have dropped and the construction
programme has been reined in, very much more significant
delays, even during the currency of some projects have been
experienced. Any medium sized company considering taking on
a project in the Middle East would be well advised to look
hard at a cash flow with payments calculated on a worst case
basis before beoming committed.

As so often is the case the officers at the University
who were supervising our project did not last the full

period of the contract. Consequently we had the difficulty of changes from the Secretary General in charge of all developments at the University down to the supervising Clerk of Works. This has to be expected in a developing nation where the nationals in the top appointments will often get early promotion and technical posts tend to be held by foreigners on limited service contracts, whether they come from the West or from Egypt, Pakistan or India.

One of the many hazzards in maintaining cash flow is the need for precise documentation without a single flaw in either the English or Arabic version. This gave us many frustrating times. Having interim valuations of perhaps £1 million or £2 million rejected because of typing errors involving only pence seems quite incredible to us, especially when the normal procedures involve re-submittal in two languages and checking at four or five different stages before payment is made. Inevitably even with the best will in the world such payments arrive late.

Living and working conditions have been transformed in the past few years. Comfortable hotels are now plentiful, telephone and telex facilities are efficient and the arrangements for importation of materials and equipment immensely improved. The difficulty of obtaining visas for expatriate employees has however substantially increased and it is frustrating to be chased by your Saudi Government client to improve progress on site whilst access to the country is delayed to the labour and supervisory personnel who could bring about the required improvement.

The importation of goods into Saudi Arabia caused us a number of headaches. We soon learnt that it was virtually impossible to import goods in our own name and we were therefore forced into the position of using either our employers name i.e. the University, or our Saudi partner's name. Like most foreign companies it took us a little while to learn this necessity and of course our suppliers had already despatched goods in the wrong name before experience showed us the problems this caused.

Importation of goods from overseas always presents the foreign contractor with some problems regarding the valuation of the goods. For example should discounts be included or not, as a higher valuation produces increased import duties and a lower valuation is likely to incur excessive profits when local taxation is assessed.

In obtaining materials it was amazing to us to find how much stock is held by suppliers in Saudi Arabia, but of course finding precisely what is mentioned in the specification locally without long term planning is an entirely different matter. The familiarity of the stockist with the goods he holds is often sketchy and it is common for your buyers to spend two or three days in the merchant's warehouse searching his stock for what is required.

The contractor has to be far more self sufficient when working overseas. There is no great wealth of local specialist sub-contractors to fall back on and so the main contractor has to cover a far greater proportion of the work. We even ended up doing mechanical and electrical work ourselves as a sub-contractor we had chosen, like so many in the area at that time, did not really have the degree of competence and financial backing necessary to achieve a tight schedule on a complicated project. We therefore took over direct responsibility for this work employing our own electricians and mechanical engineers.

Incidentially it was by no means unique to our project to find that the permanent mains electricity and water services would not be available by the time the contract completion was due. The contract works therefore had to be varied to enable temporary services to be supplied.

It took some while to acclimatize to the American type approach to contractors approval procedures which appear to have been introduced into Saudi Arabia primarily by the Corps of Engineers and the major American consultants. These required very much more attention to detail and forward planning than is normally experienced in the U.K. The procedure undoubtedly does have merit, particularly when one is working so far from home and if materials are delivered which are not acceptable, the consequences are that much more serious. The detailed forward planning necessary to satisfy such demands does have a discipline which can be usefully employed in many situations in the U.K.

On one project we carried out in Saudi Arabia however one of the largest international consultancy firms from the USA who were supervising the contract, had their employment terminated in the middle of the contract as the employer had come to the conclusion their fees were excessive.

It was a surprise to us to find that the contractor is normally expected to accept the full design liability as well as the construction liability under normal Saudi Arabian law. Any design problems which we would normally be able to shrug off under the JCT type contract may well fall on the contractor's shoulders in Saudi Arabia. With international designers from all over the world operating there, and tremendous competition from contractors to carry out construction work, it is extremely difficult to know how to handle this risk, especially as any variation proposed by the contractor to meet possible design inadequacies inevitably seems to end up with the contractor paying the additional cost involved.

When the parties to the contract come from different countries with different standards difficulties can arise. On a subsequent multi storey flat project we became involved in having to re-design the layouts originally produced by an Egyptian architect, to come some way to meeting Western fire escape requirements. This was almost unheard of at that time but many contractors have since faced serious criticism following serious fires in buildings.

The conclusion to be drawn for the medium sized contractor contemplating normal construction work in Saudi Arabia should probably be that the moment for the introduction of a newcomer has passed. More and more local contractors can cope with the medium size projects of up to £10 million or even £20 million so there is now much less scope for the foreign medium sized company. However there is still a demand for certain specialist skills, such as specialist ground exploration techniques and high quality finishes. There are also good opportunities for the maintenance and operation of Government buildings, airports, etc. These are assuming increased importance as the major building and infrastructure projects have now been completed and are reaching an age when regular planned maintenance is necessary.

Discussion on Papers 9–12

DR S.R. COCHRANE, Queen's University, Belfast

At Queen's University, I have been teaching students from Malaysia, Singapore, Hong Kong, the Middle East and African countries for over eleven years. We are now extending our courses at postgraduate level to cater for a well-defined need arising from training difficulties experienced by recent graduates in those countries. These graduates are often denied the opportunity to be trained in basic design and construction. Postgraduate courses are now being provided to bridge this gap and we offer one such MSc course at Queen's.

Dr Starr has shown how a wide-ranging education and training programme is required in many developing countries. He might have described how Construction Industry Training Boards, such as in the UK, might be formed in developing countries. I agree with Mr Duncan about the high quality of many of the Malaysian and Far Eastern students and young engineers now being produced, and would point to the need to see these young enthusiastic beginners maturing to experienced and well-trained engineers in the future.

I must take up a point made this morning with regard to micro computing being only for the under 45s. I am sure there is no reason why over 45s cannot also enjoy using word processors, spread sheets, data bases and graphics generally. I intend to do so until I am about 90.

Referring to construction management generally, I often detect a lack of forward planning and procurement at the design stage in traditional consultancy. Indeed, critical path networks may often be seen yellowing on the wall of some site offices; and in many UK design offices, the word procurement may be thought of as vaguely immoral. The use of the FIDIC red book in international multi-discipline projects sometimes leads to difficulties in relating the three controls – time, cost and quality – to each other: bills of quantities seldom 'talk to' construction programmes in an efficient manner and any revision of FIDIC might consider these weaknesses.

MR M.A. AL-MUFTI, Queen's Univerity, Belfast

Paper 9 reflects a very sensitive understanding and

appreciation of the human factors involved in the training process. In that respect, paragraph 3 touches upon the effect of the '(apparent) confidence ... of the expatriates on the morale of the professionals in the developing world'; and I would suggest adding the word 'over' before the word 'confidence'.

Another observation is with reference to paragraph 15 where it states, 'training must start from where people are, not where they should be'. Trainees may expect some form of promotion after completion of training and indeed such training may be one of the requirements of promotion. In the process, the trainee may end up being promoted out of the job for which he trained in the first place.

Mr Siberry, in the introduction to Paper 5, mentioned that some of the Algerians his company trained were subsequently promoted to higher positions, with the result that others had to be trained. Therefore, it may be important to stress to the trainees not only what their expected role is but also its importance; and to point out this phenomenon to the institutions to which they belong.

In this respect, training must start from where people are, to enable them to perform better at their present jobs; and it should not be used as a means of promoting them to where they think they ought to be, although this may be an additional bonus in the long run.

MR S.A. MURRAY, Ove Arup Partnerhip

I would like to suggest to Mr Parish that his comments on the future for consultancy are perhaps indicative of a much deeper trend in project engineering.

The execution of engineering projects requires certain basic skills. These include design, analysis, cost control, planning and construction. The traditional roles of consultant and contractor represent groupings of those skills into functional forms. These traditional roles were actually developed for the civil engineering projects of a generation ago, but over the years they have become formalised in our forms of contract, our firms and our institutions.

I suggest that what we are seeeing now is a breaking down of traditional roles and a return to basic skills. The process is caused by various factors, including,
- the clients' perception of the failure of the traditional methods on certain types of project
- the desire of clients to be selective in the services for which they pay
- straight competition.

If this process continues, the future promises to be very exciting. The challenge for us is to be the most skilful in a particular field and to be the most flexible in combining our skills in the forms most appropriate for the projects. The only question which remains is that of how we and our institutions will react to the challenge.

MR K.D. STAPLES, Watson Hawksley

With reference to Paper 10, while in considerable agreement with the Author about the changing role of the consultant, I would suggest that there is a somewhat better prospect of involvement in medium-scale projects using younger British engineers. The system of training in the UK, fostered by the ICE, provides engineers with experience in design and in the practical aspects of construction at a fairly early stage in their career. That experience can usefully cover the shortage of local engineers with practical experience, a situation likely to continue in many countries on account of the established tendency in many areas for the relatively few local engineers to be rapidly 'promoted' to administration or commercial management.

The suggestion that in turnkey projects the consultant is simply engaged by the contractor client is perhaps not entirely satisfactory. The discussion on Paper 6 (Joint Ventures) noted that consultants are not financially competent to be full risk-sharing parties. I suggested that the motivation of the consultant and his staff, and the need to demonstrate a commitment, justified a slightly more organic involvement. Would Mr Parish agree that such involvement might best be demonstrated by the consultant having some element of his financial return associated with the project profitability?

MR H.K.H. CLAXTON, Paterson Candy International

Our industry is too fragmented to permit the development of marketing strategies which target identified markets and aim to ensure that work in those markets comes to British firms. We have heard that both Japan and Korea are using the training of host country engineers as a marketing tool. No single British consultant or contractor is likely to be able to match the initiatives of Korea and Japan, and we run the risk, therefore, of delivering those markets, in the long-term, to our competition.

I am pessimistic about the ability of our consultants to respond effectively to the threats identified in Mr Parish's Paper. I am pessimistic about the ability of our contractors, acting separately, to compete with the concerted, national efforts of our competitors.

Unless the industry pools its resources in order to develop and implement imaginative marketing strategies, which are directed at specifically identified markets and employ such devices as training and locally established companies, I am pessimistic about UK (Engineering) Ltd's ability to compete in the long-term. This has consequences for British engineers, unless they wish to fulfil the role of 'hired help' to overseas consultants and contractors.

United we stand, divided we fall, but where is the mechanism or vehicle whereby we unite to compete effectively with international, and particularly Far Eastern, competitors.

MR N.R. MANSFIELD, University of Strathclyde

One point with regard to Paper 9, I agree it is especially true that overseas client countries will quickly see through attempts at providing training and instruction which either are not genuine or are ill-conceived. Having worked alongside nationals in a Central American government department, it is good to hear a systematic presentation of human resources development overseas. It would be interesting to hear any comment on the handling of conflicts and complications which do arise in many developing countries from the very real political constraints which often frustrate aspiring national engineers and managers.

Referring to Paper 10 and the changing role of consultants. At the University of Strathclyde, a sample of consulting engineering firms were contacted as part of a wider study. It was noted that over a five-year period there was a reduction of 14%, on average, in staff employed. This figure was higher for those firms with low percentages of overseas work. The most popular area of work was the Middle East followed by Africa and Asia, with very little involvement in the EEC. Firms usually acted in a lead capacity for 70% of the projects, including those at home and overseas. New problems were arising from too great a dependence on traditional markets, such as the Middle East, and from a difficulty in offering services which were markedly different from those of competitors. Future opportunities were believed to lie in the provision of specialist services, in French speaking areas and in the correct packaging of work to suit new organisational forms. The overseas local agent in the host country often proved crucial to success: selection was made either by means of a government sponsored trade mission, or by way of a local company previously known in other countries, or by direct contact built up through individual visits. Maximum information would be sought on the commercial, political and technical connections of the prospective agent, including their integrity, drive and personality. However, the final decision on the selection had to be left to the firm's or company's man-in-charge on the spot at the time. Does Mr Parish have any guide-lines to offer on the satisfactory selection of the overseas agent or partner? Is it considered that French speaking areas will prove more promising in future and is there much chance of EEC related work expanding significantly?

MR PARISH

I opened the verbal presentation of my Paper with the hope that it might be somewhat controversial and I am a little surprised, even disappointed, that this discussion has shown such a substantial level of agreement with my views.

Mr Murray has really paraphrased my thoughts in a more succinct and elegant way, which I feel calls for no further comment.

I agree with Mr Staples' point about the virtues of the

British system of education and training for civil engineers,
although I could wish that the site experience included work
as a carpenter's mate, a member of a steel-fixing gang or a
concreting gang, rather than solely as a cadet officer in the
contractor's or consultant's site organisation. However, the
usefulness of such young engineers does not change the perhaps
understandable nationalism which clearly seems to require the
use of local engineering talent. Mr Staples' point about
consultants 'standing their corner' in consortia is a
contentious one. What the consultant clearly cannot do is to
accept 'joint and several' liability with a contractor; with
say 5% of the project value he does not have the financial
resources to guarantee performance of the 95%, but he is, or
certainly should be, strong enough to carry his proportional
share of the guarantee. This 'joint and several' liability
has sunk many potential consortia of substantial contractors
and suppliers, so it is clearly not just a problem for
consultants. Certainly, I see no objection to the consultant
having his reward linked in an equitable way with project
profitability.

Mr Claxton is hoeing a very familiar row where the essential
argument is that it would be attractive to have UK Limited as
a counter-force to the national capabilities of Japan and
Korea, but the British are not really made in a way to cause
that to be possible. Many organisations, contractors and
consultants, are implementing their market strategy by
including the use of training and local companies. What I
believe to be a valuable contribution would be to break down
the wall which still exists to some applicable extent between
contractors and consultants and vice versa. Sadly, this
sniping emerged during the seminar, and the sooner we all
realise that we exist in our own fields in a highly
competitive world where co-operation is essential, the sooner
we will challenge Japan Inc. or Korea Inc.

Mr Mansfield's experience with the sample of consultancies
is not paralleled by my own firm's experience, where we have
had substantially less than a 14% reduction in staff numbers,
although our work is almost equally divided between UK and
overseas. However, I can only concur with his implicit plea
for flexibility in the services provided. Having been
involved with consultancy in francophone countries for over 20
years, I would certainly support the existence of that market
opportunity. As to agents, the emphasis on the various
considerations set out by Mr Mansfield vary from country to
country and I know of no wholly reliable way of making a
selection which will guarantee success.

Finally, I see little opportunity within the EEC for
straight forward engineering consultancy, but some
possibilities for specialist high technology and management
consultancy.

MR T.H. NICHOLSON, Consulting Engineer
    In response to comments made on the appointment of engineers

153

to contracts in the process industry, I would like to add the following.

In my experience of that industry, it had been recognised that the choice of an engineer to a contract has to achieve a balance in order that:

(a) the engineer is sufficiently involved in the contract to be able to undertake his duties under the contract in a properly informed way, and

(b) he is sufficiently senior in the employer's organisation to be able to make engineer's decisions effectively and to undertake the engineer's role.

This meant that the appointed engineer was often at Group Manager level and that more senior engineers and directors were free to undertake the role of the employer.

MR D.G. COMPSTON, Allott & Lomax

May I first congratulate Mr Duncan and Mr Try on their very interesting Papers and also congratulate their firms on the successful penetration of overseas markets.

It is very interesting to note the platforms on which these successes were based. One firm which has a very specialised expertise used this to find the entrée to the market, thereby limiting competition to gain a strong foothold, while the other firm went to the most active market and by well planned selling techniques obtained a share of that market for itself.

The problem now is that all the overseas markets have reduced in volume, although I cannot speak with particular knowledge of Hong Kong where, however, there is uncertainty about the long-term future.

We are all, therefore, having to consider where the significant overseas construction projects of the future are going to be, and from where funds to ensure payment are to be provided.

Clearly, the aid funded projects must be a focus of our attention and certainly consultants from the UK are working hard to take at least a fair share of the aid funded project market. This work is very widely spread about the world and, as Mr Parish has said, the larger projects are considerably fewer in number. There is, however, some criticism that UK contractors have not been obtaining their share of this aid funded work.

As these Papers demonstrate, it is very difficult and time-consuming to set up a contracting business away from the home base, but the UK construction industry is being urged to do more, particularly, for example, on EEC funded work. It would be interesting to have more information on the opportunities for work supported by the EEC and indeed other multi-lateral development funds.

14 The Dubai aluminium smelter project

P. D. V. MARSH, Wimpey Major Projects Ltd, London

The Dubai Aluminium Smelter Project constructed between 1977 and 1981 is not only one of the largest industrial projects ever undertaken, value $1.3 billion, but also provides material from which much can be learnt in regard to the management of overseas projects.

This paper is divided into three sections :

Section A - in which I will describe the essentials of the Project itself.

Section B - will cover the way in which the Project was conceived, finance and managed.

Section C - in which I will draw some lessons for the future.

SECTION A

In outline, the Project consisted of a 135,000 tpa aluminium smelter with its own anode manufacturing plant, a 515 MW gas fired power station complete with waste heat boilers, a 25 million gallon per day desalination plant and all ancillary facilities and related infrastructure within the 260 acre site on the Jebel Ali coastline some 30 Km from Dubai together with the unloading facilities at the Jebel Ali port. To give but two statistics, 350,000 freight tons of material were moved over 3 years, a total of 300,000 cu m of concrete were poured with a maximum weekly output of $3100m^3$ per day. The overall completion period was 52 months.

The attached chart gives the division of the Project into sub-contracts and the various consultants involved. The overall Engineers were P U Fisher and they were supported by Kennedy and Donkin as Engineers for the Power Complex and Desalination Plant and D G Jones as the Quantity Surveyors.

Project Elements

The Project was divided into 8 elements :

1. Site preparation/development, administrative buildings and interconecting services. This included the facilities for the construction work force which comprised at the peak of the construction period approximately 4,000 expatriate employees, 3,500 being third world nationals supervised by expatriate European staff. Accommodation had to be provided for all of

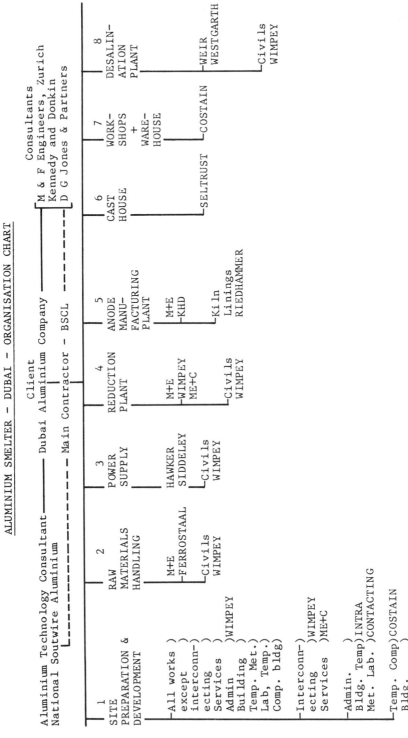

ALUMINIUM SMELTER – DUBAI – ORGANISATION CHART

these people so as not to overburden the existing facilities in the city of Dubai. Two separate accomodation camps were therefore constructed to cater for the diverse needs and cuisine of the third country nationals and the European staff. The third world national camp included its own mosque and the canteen produced up to 60,000 pieces of nan bread a day. Also within this package were included the vital electrical and mechanical interconnecting service.

2. Raw Material Handling. Raw material handling facilities are located at a dedicated berth at Jebel Ali port, constructed at the same time under a separate contract, located some 6 Kms from the smelter. These facilities comprise a movable unloader which sucks the alumina out of the ship's hold, storage silos capable of holding 5,000 tonnes of petroleum coke and alumina silos each 186 ft high and capable of holding 30,000 tonnes of alumina. Loading and unloading is controlled from a central console. The alumina is taken to site by truck.

3. Power Supply and Distribution. Continuity of power supply is vital to an aluminium smelter. If there is a loss of power lasting over 2 hours then the electrolyte within the reduction cells would start to solidify. The cost of replacing a frozen cell is about $20,000 and there are 360 of them.

Power to a total of 515 MW is provided by a combination of 5 frame 9 gas turbines of 70 MW each and 8 frame 5 gas turbines of 17.5 MW at 95°F ambient. The choice of two sizes of turbine was to provide operational flexibility. This provides a 50% stand-by capacity for the smelter, power for the Desalination Plant and for feeding into the Dubai Municipality grid. Fuel for the turbines in the form of dry gas is supplied by Dugal from an off-shore gas field after separation out from the wet gas of propane, butane and condensate which are sold separately.

The waste heat from the turbines is used in waste heat boilers to provide steam for delivery to the Desalination Plant.

4. Reduction Plant. The reduction plant in which the actual conversion of alumina to aluminium takes place is the heart of the smelter and comprises essentially 360 cells or pots located in 3 potlines. The steel pots are lined with a carbon cathode connected to the negative terminal of the bus bar system. Above the pot, pre-baked carbon anodes fitted to aluminium anode rods are clamped to a positive bus bar.

During the reduction process alumina is dissolved in a molten bath of cryolite at a temperature of about 970° C. An electric current of about 150,000 amps is passed through the bath decomposing the alumina and allowing the aluminium to form which settles at the bottom of the cell from which it is tapped about every 32 hours by a vacuum device into a crucible.

5. The Anode Plant. This comprises :
- The Green Mill where petroleum coke fractions are blended

157

with pitch and formed by vibro compaction into unbaked or "green" anodes.

- The kilns where the green blocks each weighing 850 kg are cured to a temperature of 1250°C for up to 60 hours.

- The Anode Rodding Room where the anode blocks are attached to the anode rods using a cast iron bond. When in service, each anode is consumed within 10 days and therefore with a total demand of baked anodes of 92,456 tonnes per annum, it is essential to maintain a guaranteed supply to the potrooms.

6.   The Cast House. The molten aluminium is transported in 5 ton crucibles to the cast house which contains melting furnaces, ingot and D.C. casting machines and saws for cutting slab and billet. The melting furnaces receive the molten aluminium and also scrap aluminium. The casters produce aluminium ingots, slab or billets.

7.   Workshops and Warehouses. Due to the absence of local repair facilities and the need to maintain continuous production the plant has been provided with comprehensive machine shops, paint shops and indeed are electrical, mechanical and implementation facilities needed for comprehensive maintenance purpose.

8.   Desalination. Drinking water is an essential commodity but one which natural sources are becoming less and less able to supply to meet the Gulf's increasing demand. Seawater is pumped into the plant and, using a flash evaporation process, the water is first heated by steam and then passed through a series of chambers each at a lower pressure and temperature than the last, in each of which the vapour after passing through demisters to remove salt water droplets, condenses and is collected as fresh water.

The plant output is 25 million gallons per day. Of this only half a million is needed for the Smelter and the rest is available for the township of Dubai.

SECTION B

Project Conception

The Dubai Smelter was conceived by two entrepreneurs; Sheikh Rashid Bin Saeed Al Makhtoum, the Ruler of Dubai, and Paul Brauner, the Chairman of BSCL. BSCL (British Smelter Constructions Limited) was then a company owned 50% by George Wimpey and 50% Selection Trust and had been responsible for the constructon of the aluminium smelter at Bahrein starting in 1968 and taking just over 2 years to construct. The Project's birth was made feasible by a set of possibly unique circumstances. (The Ruler had control over the source and price of power which normally accounts for about 30% of a smelter's operating costs.) As the development of Dubai as a major city, and the industrialisation of Jebel Ali proceeded, there was going to be a serious shortage of water and the essential steam for the desalination plant could be provided at minimal cost utilising waste heat from the smelter power station. There could be no environmental objections as the plant is quite simply in the desert, although environmentally

it is in fact designed and operated to the highest standards
and excellent pollution control has been achieved by Dubal.)
(The key decisions were in the hands not of committees, but of
one man, the Ruler of Dubai. Smelters do not demand large
work forces to operate and this suits a country in which the
work force has almost wholly to be imported and it suits the
competitiveness of the smelter which is not burdened by
expensive over-manning.

So the Project was right in its utilisation of power, in its
dual function as a producer of aluminium and water, in its
role as part of the country's industrialisation programme and
environmentally.)

It had undeniable appeal as the development the Ruler wanted
and the sort of a scheme which the Chairman of BSCL wanted to
see built.

Finance

Initially the Project was wholly financed by loans provided
against the guarantee of the Dubai Government.
These loans were of 3 types :

1. An ECGD Buyer Credit to finance the provision of the
goods and services from the UK.

2. A Eurodollar loan to finance front end and local costs
together with other non-sterling payments.

3. A German suppler credit to cover the German portion.

The possibility of project financing was considered but not
proceeded with due to the difficulties involved of entering
into off-take agreements so far ahead in time which were
adequate to provide a sufficient degree of loan security.

During the period of the contract the amounts covered by
these loans proved insufficient and Dubal arranged the
necessary extra finance principally in the form of additional
loans.

There are 2 key points to be noted in relation to the
financing :

1. The willingness of the UK and German export credit
agencies to provide financial support necessarily dictated the
countries of supply.

2. Because of the size of the Project and ECGD's
requirements on recourse, it was necessary to break the main
contract down into a limited number only of major sub-
contracts each of which was itself the responsibility of a
substantial company.

Management

The management of the Project evolved as the organisational
structures of the Client, the Dubai Aluminium Company (Dubal),
and of BSCL themselves developed and expanded to meet the
Project's needs.

When the order was place in May 1976 the Client, Dubal, did
not even exist. When the Project began on site in February
1977 the Client's organisation was still embryonic and he was
heavily reliant on his various consultants. As the job
proceeded Dubal increasingly came to take charge of the

Project both technically, commercially and financially. A significant factor in the changing managerial role of Dubal was that the starting-up of the first potline began on schedule in November 1979 but final completion was not scheduled until May 1981. That meant Dubal had to have their operating management team in place some 2 years prior to completion the effect of which was that construction and operations were proceeding in parallel so Dubal's involvement in construction management necessarily increased to take account of the inter-action between the operation of one part of the Smelter to the completion and commissioning of others.

On the contractor's side the crucial decision was that taken about half way through the contract to shift control to site both for construction and commercially.

Civil engineering companies are accustomed to controlling major jobs from site but this is much less true of firms who are electrical and mechanical manufacturers and erectors. This difference is reflected in their methods of operation and the level of staff they place on site. It was accentuated in Dubai by reason of all the principle sub-contractors being located in Western Europe and the job being wholly financed from there. But with a level of work running at around $30m a month there was only one place at which all but the most major policy decisions could be taken and that was site. The wisdom of that decision was demonstrated by the fact of all completion targets being met and indeed the final aluminium potlines producing 3 months ahead of schedule.

SECTION C
Lessons from the Project

1.   When the Contractor is involved in project creation there is a need to distinguish carefully between his activities as a promoter and as a contractor.

2.   The need to establish at the time of contract signature an effective client organisation.

3.   The desirability to minimise the number of consultants reporting directly to the Client.

4.   The need to recognise the risks assumed by a main contractor, even when his direct work is limited to management of the project, when differing legal practicalities govern the relationship between himself and the client and himself and his sub-contractors.

5.   Physical difficulties such as a harsh environment and the lack of local back-up are easier to overcome than those relating to people.

6.   Project control must be concentrated at site at the earliest opportunity.

7.   The desirability of avoiding very large sub-contact packages with a number of levels of different sub-contractors' management, particularly where the sub-sub-contractors are such that they can have direct relations with the Client

8.   That if the Project itself is fundamentally right for the country concerned, that it can withstand the shocks to which over a five year period it will inevitably be subject.

15 Management of civil engineering contract at Torness

W. C. JONES and D. C. WEATHERSEED, Sir Robert McAlpine and Sons Ltd, London

SYNOPSIS. The Nuclear Power Station which the South of Scotland Electricity Board are building at Torness, near Dunbar, is based on the British designed Advanced Gas-Cooled Reactor (A.G.R.). A Preliminary Contract was awarded to Sir Robert McAlpine and Sons, Ltd. in February 1979 to prepare the site which included the reclamation of 60 acres of land from the sea, building a new sea wall, besides preparing a greenfield site for the multidiscipline project which was to follow. This was then followed by the award of the Main Civil Engineering Works Contract which involved the placing of $650,000m^3$ of concrete, 50,000 tonnes of reinforcement and $900,000m^2$ of formwork. To achieve this in the programme period it was necessary to assemble a workforce of some 2,700 men at peak together with a staff of 385. The total value of the Civil Works Contracts were around £200M based on 1979 prices.

INTRODUCTION

1. The Management of any Contract, whatever its size and complexity, is dependent on Team Work for its success. The size of the project and length of programme dictate the number of men and amount of plant required.

2. Plant is the least of the problems - provided the right "Tool" for the job is used, properly maintained, and manned, the work will be carried out efficiently. But by far the most complex problems that arise are those affecting the workforce, i.e. the human problems, all of which require detailed attention to ensure a happy, efficient and motivated workforce.

3. Consequently the Management of a large project, such as Torness, spend a considerable part of their time sorting out these human relation problems and hence the greater part of this talk will be dealing with that side of the Management responsibilities rather than the engineering.

4. Torness is located on the Lothian Coastline about 7 km south of Dunbar adjacent to the main trunk road A1. There is no rail link to the site so that Civil Works were dependent entirely on road transportation. East Lothian is an agri-

cultural district and hence sparsley populated with few
engineering facilities available.

McALPINE SITE ORGANISATION

5. It has always been the McAlpine policy to make each
Contract autonomous. The Project Manager, together with his
site staff, is fully responsible for carrying out the Works as
well as administering the needs of the two Management Contracts
of the common site service facilities.

6. The Agent is responsible for administering the everyday
running of the Contract with the aid of the Section Heads and
their respective teams, covering all the necessary disciplines
required by a Contractor's Organisation.

7. Although all decisions are made from the site, the site
staff have the back-up of the Head Office Organisation, if
required. Particular mention must be made of the Accounts,
Design Office, Plant and Buying Departments and the Concrete
and Testing Laboratory.

8. The site is divided into sections, each with its own
team of Engineers, who are responsible for all the technical
aspects of the work, whereas the Works Manager controls the
men and plant necessary for executing the work.

9. The Key Personnel positions are always filled from
inside the Company but inevitably, as on any large contract,
some staff will need to be recruited. Numerous applications
for employment are always being received throughout the
duration of a contract and hence shortages are rarely known
on a prestigious project.

10. In the case of the workforce, personnel known to individuals or who have worked for the Company in the past, if
available, will be encouraged to come back.

11. Technical Staff at a junior level can be supplemented by
employing Engineering College Students who require industrial
training as part of their Degree Course. They provide a
valuable contribution to a project and benefit immensely from
the wide range of experience available to them.

12. Specialist staff may be provided by Agencies which are
a valuable source to meet short-term requirements.

13. It is necessary for Companies to acknowledge that the
conditions in which staff operate on a large Multi-Contract
site will be very different from those operating on a
Company's smaller Contracts. This applies to works and
technical staff alike many of whom often find it difficult to
be a member in a large team.

14. Bringing a large number of staff into an area will
inevitably produce accommodation problems. As many staff will
not want to uproot their families, they will be seeking
lodgings in an area which is already experiencing difficulty
providing accommodation for the labour force. Many Companies
find purchasing properties and running them as Staff Hostels a
satisfactory solution as the establishment can be run to suit
their particular requirements specially with regard to working
hours.

15. The placement and organisation of the Technical Staff is different from that of the Works Staff. The Technical Staff will be allocated to an area or section and they will be responsible for the engineering within that section, but will have the support of a central administration and of specialist groups. However, Works Staff will tend to be supervising trade groups and, therefore, will be allocated to whichever section requires their particular expertise. Continuity within a section must be maintained by having a permanent Section Foreman. This system has considerable advantages over the alternative of completely autonomous sections as it concentrates the expertise and allows the overall resources to be employed more efficiently.

16. No organisation can exist without a commercial section. Their responsibilities are varied but Timekeeping, Wages and Bonus sections are closely allied to those of the Industrial Relations and Welfare scene. The clerical side increases in numbers as the project builds up but does not decrease in the same proportions as the work load is reduced.

17. In a large organisation which has to evolve quickly, it is necessary for the Site Management to get the system right the first time. A large part of Management's function is communication and the Supervisory Staff provide this line of communication. It is, therefore, essential that Staff are engaged early to allow proper attention to be paid to the establishment of effective procedures and systems of work.

LABOUR

18. The Client recognised a need and built a Construction Village at Innerwick, close to the site, with accommodation for 640 manual and supervisory staff. Caravan facilities were also provided for men to bring their wives and families.

19. As our demands for specialist labour could not be fulfilled locally, the workforce has been recruited from many parts of the country. At its peak, our workforce exceeded 2,700 No., of which approximately 50% required temporary local accommodation. As the Construction Village could only cater for a small percentage and local accommodation was limited, many were obliged to find digs as far afield as Edinburgh, more than 30 miles from Torness. Public transport in the area was also inadequate to convey the personnel to site, and therefore, private arrangements had to be made to provide transport from as far as Edinburgh to the North and Berwick-on-Tweed to the South. Provision had also to be made to convey those accommodated in the Construction Village. Because of the nature of the work being undertaken on a 24 hour per day basis, provision for those working unsocial hours had also to be made.

20. The Project has made a great impact on the local inhabitants and business people who, before work at Torness commenced, had become accustomed only to catering for the needs of holiday-makers visiting the areas for a few months of the year. The large influx of workers recruited from outwith the

area, being temporary residents, although bringing much needed
prosperity to the area, also added to the social problems.
This, in addition to the nature of the Project, has caused the
locals some concern, making it necessary to foster good public
relations.

INDUSTRIAL RELATIONS

21. Government Enactments over the last two decades have seen
the introduction of a welter of Statutes which now form the
framework of Industrial Legislation. No Industry is more aware
of its effects and implications than the labour intensive
Construction Industry. Any large Multi-Contractor Engineering
Construction Project which relies heavily on an operative force
of thousands, is a potential Industrial Relations nightmare
unless adequate machinery exists to facilitate negotiation and
conciliation. Considerable emphasis is placed upon Management
to draw up good Industrial Relations Policies and to ensure
that those responsible for its application understand its implications and apply it systematically and with consistency.

22. Most major Engineering Construction Sites are Multi-
farious in activity but can generally be divided into two
elements:

> (a) The Civil Engineering Construction element which
>   can embrace a multitude of 'finishing' activities.

> (b) The Plant Engineering Construction facet which
>   embraces such work as Mechanical and Electrical
>   installation, structural steel supply and erection
>   and so forth.

The Civil Engineering Industry is overseen nationally by the
Civil Engineering Construction Conciliation Board for Great
Britain, constituted by an Employers Federation and three
signatory Trade Unions. This body is responsible for determining employment conditions for Civil Engineering operatives
and provides a facility for resolving Industrial Disputes
which cannot be resolved locally. Employment conditions are
published in the Board's National Working Rule Agreement.

23. The Plant Engineering Construction Industry is similarly
organised by a National Joint Council with its own published
Agreement on Employment Conditions. The Council is representative of two employer bodies and seven signatory Trade
Unions.

24. Unlike the Working Rules for the Civil Engineering
Industry, which permits but does not encourage local Agreements, the National Agreement for the Engineering Construction
Industry makes provision for the 'Nomination' of certain
projects, and the large Multi-Contractor project will invariably be classified accordingly.

25. Once a project has been 'Nominated', a Supplementary
Project Agreement is negotiated between the participating
Companies, whose activities are within scope of the National
Agreement and their employees' Trade Union Officials, to

164

embrace the particular coniditions of employment, negotiating
and disciplinary procedures which will apply to that project.
Terms negotiated under a Project Agreement are supplementary
and complementary to those of the National Agreement for
Engineering Construction and must be approved by the National
body before adoption.

26. Additionally under the 'Nomination' procedure a Project
Joint Council is formed, the membership of which is similarly
drawn from the participating 'In Scope' Contractors and their
employees' Trade Union Representatives. Each side will
nominate a Chairman, with a Secretary nominated by the
National Council.

27. The Project Joint Council's purpose is to uphold the
Terms of the National Agreement, together with the additional
Supplementary Project Agreement in the areas of Pay and
Conditions, Health, Safety and Welfare and the promotion of
good standards of productivity, all with a view to developing
and maintaining good Industrial Relations.

28. Many of the Companies engaged on the larger Multi-
Contractor projects are not party to or within scope of the
Project Joint Council and the Project Agreements, the
principal exclusion being the Main Civil Engineering
Contractor and many of his specialist Sub-Contractors.

29. Apart from his own responsibilities, the Main Civil
Engineering Contractor must assume responsibility for the
well-being of the employees of his many Sub-Contractors, by
ensuring that their procedures, such as Labour and Safety
Policies are thoroughly vetted and approved, and also that
effective measures are introduced to ensure the satisfactory
maintenance of those Policies.

30. Where there is interface and inter-relationship between
the activities and employees of the participating contractors,
areas of possible conflict may emerge. Therefore, some co-
ordinating body must be introduced to implement an effective
control and correlation of activities common to the majority
of those contractors, particularly in the area of earnings
potential.

31. Considerable emphasis is placed by operatives on earnings
potential under 'second tier' or bonus incentive payments.
It is desirable that as many employees as possible should be
covered by such bonus incentive and it is imperative that any
scheme should be based on sound, well tried targets which will
permit acceptable bonus earnings related to measured
productivity. In view of the wide variations which exist in
basic wage rates, considerable 'over-emphasis' can often be
applied to this element of earnings and it is essential that
adequate monitoring of 'pay and performance' levels is carried
out in order to ensure a degree of compatibility amongst the
many trades people who, by the nature of their work, have an
affinity to each other.

32. Another area which can often breed discontent is in the
provision of welfare facilities. Standards often vary widely
from contractor to contractor and a sensible client on a major

project, recognising the dangers of inconsistency amongst the many Contractors, will introduce his own 'common user' facilities e.g. camp and canteen, toilets and medical needs, thus ensuring a satisfactory level of facility at all times.

33. In order to oversee the whole Industrial Relation scene at Torness, a Management Group has been formed. This Group is chaired by an independent Chairman and is made up generally of Representatives at Director level of all the major Contractors. The meetings are held off site at two monthly intervals, but the Group can be called together at any time should occasion demand. The main function of this Group, besides establishing a sound Industrial Relations Policy, is to acquaint all Companies of the basic Rules applying to the site such as Safety, Security, Construction Village etc. All decisions arrived at by the Management Group apply to all Contractors on site. The Group has various Sub-Committees which examine Contractors' policies such as Conditions of Employment, Bonus Schemes and Safety and these must be approved before a Contractor commences work.

THE EFFECT ON THE SOCIAL AND ENVIRONMENTAL FABRIC OF A COMMUNITY RESULTING FROM THE IMPORTATION OF LABOUR

34. Many major Civil Engineering Projects are carried out in areas remote from the larger conurbations and in the absence of an immediately available labour force within the locality, the import of non-local workers is necessary. On a project which requires labour measured in thousands, the sudden introduction of operatives in such numbers inevitably places an immediate strain on the social and environmental fabric of the local community. The nature of the intended project can determine to a large extent the ease or difficulty with which the arrival of the Client and his Contractor can be accepted by the local community.

35. Invariably, Heavy Civil Engineering Projects are socially necessary, but, to many, socially unacceptable. Projects such as Oil Refineries or Power Stations are an essential service to the community at large but the immediate and direct benefits to the local community are not always instantly recognised or appreciated. To many, benefits of any kind are of no interest or consolation when the intended project, be it Oil Refinery, Power Station or whatever, is an anathema, an intrusion in their community and socially and ecologically unacceptable.

36. It is into this often somewhat hostile environment that the Contractor has to introduce himself and his large labour force. The immediate need is for suitable accommodation and this requirement can be quite varied. Inevitably, in the more isolated areas, suitable and adequate accommodation is at a premium and, on the basis of the supply and demand principle, rental charges can quickly become exorbitant. Consideration has to be given, therefore, to the building of a construction camp which is, in itself, a major exercise and fraught with all the usual planning difficulties. Substantial benefits

can be gained, however, in the provision of a construction camp, for with sensible siting in terms of location, a great deal of pressure can be removed from the existing community.

37. The extent of the facilities available within the community will determine very much the level to which the provision of services within the camp will extend but such services as Medical Centres, Laundry, Recreational Facilities are invariably essential. However, it is beneficial where existing services are available, namely Library, Churches and Social Clubs, that the labour force should be able to utilise these in the hope that the integration with the local community will foster good relations. This is not always the case initially, but experience has shown that with the passage of time the non-local element of the labour force can settle down within a community and make a positive contribution, the principal benefits being job opportunities and consumer spending.

TRANSPORT

38. The geographic location of the operative labour will largely determine the need for, or desirability of, providing transport to and from the site. With a construction camp located in close proximity to the site, then no provision need necessarily be made. However, as the distance from the camp to site increases so consideration needs to be given to the provision of transport. Similarly, where a large labour force is required to be drawn from a radius up to daily travelling distance from the site, again the provision of transport has to be considered. With many major Civil Engineering Projects located in more remote areas, public transport is generally limited, if at all available, and unless public transport undertakings are prepared to supplement their services to meet the peak needs of starting and finishing times, then they cannot be a consideration.

39. In the absence of his own fleet, the hire of coaches from local coach companies is necessary. Most coach operators are attracted to this form of hire because the greater part of the Contract is carried out during early morning and evening hours thus leaving the coach free to carry out other hires during the intervening daytime. In providing any form of transport service, the Contractor must ensure that the conditions of use by his labour force, particularly with regard to time lost coming to or going from the place of work brought about by non-arrival of transport, late arrival and mechanical breakdowns, are clearly determined. If the Contractor is to avoid claims for compensation, he must disclaim liability at the outset and accept only the obligation to reimburse his operatives the requisite travel allowance, in accordance with the Terms of the Working Rule Agreement.

40. Many advantages can be gained by an Employer utilising hired transport. With coaches carrying passengers approximately equivalent to 10-15 private cars, parking congestion can be eased substantially, particularly where the coaches are

not retained on site during the working day. This benefit is extended into the local community insofar as congestion on approach roads can be eased substantially. An added benefit for an Employer when a large proportion of his labour force is conveyed to and from site on hired transport is that late arrival and early leaving during the working day is largely obviated.

THURSTON GARDENS VILLAGE, CANTEENS AND SNACK BARS

41. The above facilities are provided by the South of Scotland Electricity Board for the workforce employed on the Torness Project. A Caterer was appointed by the Board and a separate Contract was placed with Sir Robert McAlpine and Sons, Ltd. to manage the appointed Caterer and carry out other various services on site. Thurston Gardens Village is situated 3 miles from the construction site and transport to and from the works is provided by Contractors for their own personnel. Accommodation is provided for 640 men. The sleeping quarters are in chalet blocks with 20 rooms to each chalet. Every resident has his own private bedroom with wash-basin, whilst washing and toilet facilities are provided to each dormitory block. The Administrative/Amenity Block consists of:

(a) Catering Contractors Offices

(b) Reception Area

(c) 4 No. T.V. Lounges to cater for all T.V. Channels

(d) Staff Dining Room (Waitress Service), Operatives Dining Room (Self-Service)

(e) Medical Centre (Nurse on duty 24 hours daily)

(f) "Quiet" Room

(g) Video Viewing Room

(h) Operatives Bar

(i) Cabaret and Games Room

(j) Staff Bar and Games Room

(k) Gymnasium and Sports Hall and Football Field

42. All Social and Recreational activities are operated through the Thurston Gardens Social Club which is a properly constituted Club with legal bindings. It is non-profit making and all residents become Associated Members when entering the Village. The Management Committee of the Club consists of a Chairman, Secretary, Treasurer and a Committee of three. One third of the number is appointed by the Catering Contractor and two thirds are appointed by the residents. There is a Residents Committee with representatives from Contractors who have residents in the Village. The object of this Committee is to ensure that a mutually satisfactory service is maintained by a regular exchange of views relating to social

events, sport and recreation, accommodation and catering. A
Management Committee for employee facilities is established
comprising the Site Managers of the major Contractors on site
and the Board's Site Management. This Committee determines
all matters of policy and prices to be charged at the Construction Village, Site Canteens and Snack Bars.

43. As the work progressed and the workforce numbers increased
it was found necessary to operate staggered lunch breaks at
the Main Canteen, in spite of the provision of two Snack Bars.
With the coming of the Mechanical Contractors to site, who
were working a double dayshift, the whole aspect of opening
hours of the canteens, both on site and at the Village, had
to be reviewed and a new schedule of opening times drawn up.

44. The standard of accommodation set and amenities provided
at Thurston Gardens Village and the site canteens, is
excellent and must be the norm for any future major
construction site.

SUB-CONTRACTORS

45. Over 100 Sub-Contractor Orders have been placed by
McAlpine on this site of which only 4 were Nominated, the
workforces of these Companies on site ranging from 400 to 2.
The managing of Sub-Contractors is an important function of
the Main Contractor whatever the size of the Contract.
Programming the Sub-Contractors' work so that it is co-
ordinated with the overall progression of work as a whole is
just one facet. Allocating areas for workshops, stores,
drying/Mess huts and the provision of electricity and water
are among the other numerous items that have to be considered.
Due to the size and complexities of construction and design,
there are inevitably numerous meetings involving the Sub-
Contractors' operations and it is essential that the Main
Contractor is always represented to ensure that the Contract
is being adhered to. Where necessary, an Engineer or
Engineers are appointed by the Main Contractor to liaise full
time with the Sub-Contractor to co-ordinate the works. This
was particularly necessary with our Structural Steelwork
Contractor as all our tower cranes had to be made available
for steelwork erection before the Civil Works were finished.

ACQUISITION OF MATERIALS FOR THE PRODUCTION OF CONCRETE

46. Prior to the onset of a Contract during which it could
be foreseen that over $500,000m^3$ concrete would be required,
it was necessary to evaluate the possible sources of materials
as to their capability to produce the quantities required at
the quality defined in the Technical Specification. No
problems existed with the supply of cement as Works at Dunbar
were within five miles of the site. The Pulverised Fuel Ash
available from Longannet Power Station was the only acceptable
source of supply. Some shortages were experienced during the
Contract. These shortages were generally the result of the
variable demand for electricity that exists and the policy of

169

the Generating Boards that ash is only a waste product. The
supply of water-reducing plastisizer and other admixtures was
of little concern other than ensuring sufficient identifiable
tankage was available on site.

47. To obtain the quantity of coarse aggregate required, it
was necessary to place orders with two quarries capable of
producing such quantities of coarse aggregate having suitable
characteristics. As it was most likely that the coarse
aggregate would be crushed rock, a single source of natural
sand had to be found. As the aggregate quarries and the source
of P.F.A. were over fifty miles from the site, it was necessary
to arrange that the daily input to site was along agreed routes
so that the least disturbance to the local environment was
caused. These routes ensured that each Supplier used individual routes as far as possible to and from the site. The
handling of about a hundred loads of concrete materials each
day on site was undertaken by the Concrete Technical Staff as
part of their duties. On site, sufficient storage of all
materials was maintained to ensure that the production of
concrete was continuous, both day and night, and short-term
outside influences had little or no effect.

PROGRAMME

48. The Civil Engineering Programme was drawn up in 1979, at
the time of Tender and now four years into the Contract period,
the works are on programme. The Programme was based on our
previous performance whilst building Hinkley 'B' and Hunterston
'B' Nuclear Power Stations, also A.G.R's which were very
similar to Torness.

QUALITY ASSURANCE

49. This is one of the first major Civil Engineering Projects
in the country where it was made a Condition of Contract that
Quality Assurance was to be applied to the works. This involved the writing of a Quality Manual, together with all the
attendant documentation that was required. The Company has
Manuals of Instruction covering the execution of work
particularly in the concreting field, hence these documents
had to be formalised. The preparation of Quality Documents
involved many people and was a task that took a long time. It
has been found necessary, in the light of experience, to
continually update one's documentation and Works Procedures to
ensure compatibility amongst all the interested parties.
Quality Assurance was not only completely new to our Company
but to most of our Sub-Contractors who had to be guided along
to ensure that the necessary paperwork and qualifications were
met, before they could start work, even in their own works let
alone on site. Quality Assurance has caught up with everyone
on site and like "Safety" it is everyones responsibility.

COMMON SITE SERVICES

50. At the beginning of the project, McAlpine were awarded

two Management Contracts, Site Security and Site Services. The former is self-explanatory but the latter covers the management of all the common site facilities and is administered by an Office Manager and a workforce of 36. The services provided under cover of this Contract are:

1. The Management of a Nominated Sub-Contractor for the operation of Thurston Gardens Village, Main Site Canteen and Snack Bars.

2. Maintenance of Sanitation facilities

3. Maintenance of Temporary Water Supply

4. Provision and Operation of Fire Fighting facilities

5. Provision and Operation of Medical Centre

6. Office Cleaning for the Client and his Consultants

7. Pest Control

8. Operation of Waste Tip

9. Operation of Weighbridge

10. Provision of Skips - the skips to be strategically located throughout the site into which all Contractors will be required to dump their general rubbish

11. Road Cleaning and Watering, Car Parks

12. Weed Control and Maintain Grassed Areas

SAFETY

51. The Health and Safety at Works Act of 1974 requires Employers to Safeguard the Health, Safety and Welfare of all its employees, and all persons likely to be affected by its operations. Achieving this objective in the context of a large construction site involving Companies who are contract-ually unrelated, is difficult. The onus is on the Client or his Managers to produce a Site Safety Policy, defining areas of responsibilities, line of communication and procedures for ensuring adequate liaison between Contractors. In addition to requiring Contractors to comply with all Statutory Regulations, the Site Safety Policy will require Contractors to submit statements of their Company's Safety Policy. It will dictate under what circumstances a Resident Safety Officer should be appointed or whether regular visits by a Company Safety Officer will be sufficient. It will require a senior member of each Contractors Staff to be nominated to resolve matters of safety. Also all Contractors will be required to hold regular internal Safety Meetings.

52. A Contractor, with a large labour force and many Sub-Contractors, will find having separate meetings with his Sub-Contractors and Safety Representatives more managable and effective. All meetings should be formal with Agendas and

Minutes issued. In the case of the meeting with the Safety Representatives, it is necessary that each Company deals only with its own Safety Representatives and a Constitution is agreed between the parties. The Safety Representatives should be given lines of communication and encouraged to take up problems with the responsible management as and when they arise. Inevitably, the majority of Sub-Contractors employed by a Main Contractor will be of a specialist nature and it is important that their methods of working are monitored continually. Discussion at a Safety Meeting will resolve interface problems and evolve safe systems of work. Training and safety promotion should also be included in the Agenda.

53. A central feature of the Site Safety Policy will be the establishment of a Management Co-ordination Safety Committee composed of Senior Representatives of the Client, Consultants and major Contractors, along with their respective Safety Officers. It is desirable that the Committee Members should be restricted to those Companies with the most involvement. The Members of the Committee should report to their respective managements on the proceedings of their own Safety Meetings. An important function will be to investigate accident causes and accident trends and establish a positive site approach to training and safety promotion. The Committee will be able to advise on the running of the shared services, First Aid, Ambulance and Fire and Rescue Services. Site tidiness and lighting are two subjects which cause considerable concern to Site Managements. Untidiness is a major contributory factor to many site accidents. Inevitably, construction work produces a vast amount of rubbish and although each Contractor must be responsible for keeping his working area tidy, he is helped considerably if there is a central agency which, on request, provides skips for the removal and disposal of rubbish. Surveillance of housekeeping generally can be achieved by allocating areas to individual Contractors who will have the duty to monitor safety standards in their areas.

CONCLUSION

54. We have mentioned in our talk just a few of the varying subjects that are dealt with by Management each day. These are all so different but the one common aspect to all Management's problems is communication. Department heads must see and speak to one another very frequently so as to keep abreast of the latest situation. The Civil Engineering Industry's strength lies in its ability to meet changing situations rapidly. Although we are living in a computer age, the Industry still relies heavily on the human-being to get the work done.

16 The non-technical aspects of developing a major mine

T. H. LEWIS, RTZ Corporation PLC, London

SYNOPSIS

1. The aim of this paper is to discuss those aspects which must be addressed when developing a major mine and which are outside the direct sphere of engineering and construction works. The subjects covered are those to do with finance and marketing, the impact of the project on the host country during construction, environmental problems and sociological issues.

2. Obviously the somewhat cavalier division of a project into "technical" and "non-technical" areas is arbitrary and for the convenience of presentation. In practice there is a great deal of overlap and inter-relationship between these and there must be close liaison between the various disciplines.

3. The paper has been based on a real and specific project as it is felt that this gives a sharper focus. The project chosen is the Cerro Colorado copper deposit located in the Republic of Panama.

BACKGROUND INFORMATION

4. Before embarking on the main subject of this paper, it might prove useful to give some background information on the Republic of Panama and the copper deposit so as to give a perspective to the project.

The Republic of Panama

5. Panama is the most easterly of the countries located in the narrow isthmus which joins North and South America. Its immediate neighbours are Costa Rica to the west and Colombia to the east. It is famous, of course, for the Panama Canal which passes through the centre of the country linking the Atlantic and Pacific Oceans.

6. Panama is a small country by international standards. It has a land area approximately equal to 30% of the United Kingdom and its population at 1,825,000 (1980) is around 70% of that of Greater Manchester. Some 20% of the population lives in the capital, Panama City, which is also the administrative and commercial centre.

7. The gross domestic product was $3.4 billion in 1980 and around 75% of this came from the service and agricultural sectors. The overall trade deficit was some $1 billion in 1981 although there was surplus of $0.5 billion earned from services.

8. The official currency is the Balboa and this is pegged at parity with the US Dollar. However, there are no Balboa bank notes in circulation and in practice US dollar notes and coins are used together with Balboa coins.

9. Thus Panama is a small country whose main source of income is in providing services of which the most important are the Canal, Banking (there are some 127 banks represented in the Country) and the Colon Duty-Free Zone. In common with most developing countries it has a high level of external debt which amounted to some $2.6 billion as at July 1982.

10. A major aim of the Government is to discover a source of income which would balance the service sector and which would provide a long term source of benefits and jobs. The development of the Cerro Colorado copper deposit is seen as a major opportunity to realise this ambition.

The Cerro Colorado Copper Deposit

11. History. The deposit was first discovered by the Sinclair Oil company in the 1930's. Some preliminary exploration was carried out by geologists of the Panama Canal Company in the 1950's. In 1965, studies were carried out on the economic feasibility of mining the deposit as part of a country wide survey of Panamanian mineral resources conducted by the Government.

12. Canadian Javelin Limited acquired the mineral concessions for the area in 1970. In 1975, the Panamian Government recovered the concession and asked Texasgulf Inc. to assess the deposit. Texasgulf and CODEMIN - an agency of the Panamanian Government - entered into an agreement to undertake the assessment, development and operation of a mine at Cerro Colorado. Texasgulf and CODEMIN formed a company - Empresa de Cobre Cerro Colorado SA (CCSA) owned 20% by Texasgulf and 80% by CODEMIN and a pre-feasibility study was carried out.

13. In 1980, the Rio Tinto-Zinc Corporation PLC (RTZ) was invited by the Panamanian Government to involve itself in the project and, by agreement, acquired the 20% interest held by Texasgulf and a further 29% interest from CODEMIN to give the present ownership of CCSA of 51% CODEMIN and 49% RTZ.

14. During the period mid-1980 to mid-1982, RTZ spent some $25 million assessing the project. In mid-1982 with deteriorating copper prices and markets, CODEMIN and RTZ decided that the project was not economically feasible and it was placed on care and maintenance - a state in which it still remains and which is likely to continue for some time.

15. <u>The Deposit</u>. The Cerro Colorado deposit is located 250 km west of Panama City in the province of Chiriqui. The deposit is in mountainous country on the south side of the Continental Divide. Elevations in the area range between 650 metres and 1750 metres above sea level. Rainfall averages about 4200 mm in an eight month period from mid April to mid December. The remaining four months are dry with frequent wind gusts of up to 140 km per hour.

16. The ore body is a typical, highly fractured porphyry which has been outlined over an area of 2200m by 1500m. The top of the mineralisation is at an elevation of 1370m and the ore extends down to at least 110m above sea level. The in situ mineral inventory indicates total reserves of 1.4 billion tonnes of ore at an average grade of 0.78% based on a cut off grade of 0.4%. It is, by any standards, a very large resource.

17. The deposit is located in rugged terrain with steep-sided mountain valleys and torrential streams. The area is subject to very heavy annual rainfall with brief intense storms. Landslides and washouts are a continual threat and there is a history of moderate seismic activity. Present surface access to the site is by means of a 35km unsealed road with steep grades.

18. The studies carried out so far have considered mine sizes ranging from 8 million tonnes of ore a year up to about 40 million tonnes of ore a year. If one takes account of overall economics, risks, and marketing and financing constraints, the most likely size at the moment seems to be in the range of 15 to 20 million tonnes of ore per year. A mine of this size together with a mill and concentrator and the necessary infrastructure and power supplies, would cost around $1 billion to $1.25 billion in today's values, excluding inflation and interest during construction.

19. The construction time would be about 3 to 4 years but construction would not start until a detailed feasibility study had been carried out including bulk sampling of the ore and building a pilot plant. This feasibility study would cost some $75 million to $100 million and take around 1 to 2 years.

20. Some of the statistics for a mine of this size are interesting. As an illustration, a mine processing a nominal 50,000 tonnes per day of ore has been used.

- The life of the mine, based on the present reserves would be around forty years.

- Some 85 million tonnes of overburden would have to removed to expose the ore body.

- The mine would produce some 16.5 million tonnes of ore each year. The total amount of material to be mined – including overburden and waste rock would average some

40 million tonnes a year.

- There would be approximately 480,000 tonnes of copper concentrate produced each year.

- The electric power required by the mine, mill concentrator and associated infrastructure would be about 80 MW.

- The construction workforce would peak at around 3700 and some 1700 people would be employed during operations.

NON-TECHNICAL ASPECTS

Introduction

21. The purpose of this paper is to discuss the non-technical aspects which have to be addressed when considering a project of this size. This is not to belittle the technical problems; these represent a demanding challenge in their own right. The distinction between "technical" and "non-technical" aspects is mainly one of convenience. In reality there is a great deal of overlap and choices made in the technical area can have a large effect on the non-technical aspects and vice-versa.

22. The non-technical area can be further divided into the following subjects.

a. Financial and Marketing

b. The Impact on Panama

c. Environmental

d. Sociological

23. Again, there is a great deal of inter-relation between these and the overall approach during the planning phase has to be step-by-step taking account of all factors.

Financial and Marketing Aspects

24. It was stated above that the likely costs in today's values would be around $1 billion to $1.25 billion. If inflation and interest costs during construction are included, the total out-turn cost would be around $2 billion and this is the sum which would have to be raised by the partners.

25. Neither the government of Panama nor RTZ would raise sums this large as their own equity or under their own guarantees. It would be essential for the bulk of the money to be raised as limited recourse loans whereby the lenders would be repaid out of the proceeds of the project.

26. On the assumption that the project would be financed 30% by equity and 70% by limited recourse loans, Panama and RTZ would have to find some $600 million, split 51% Panama and 49% RTZ, with $1400 million being lent by banks, export credit agencies, etc.

27. The limited recourse loans would only be available if the lenders could be convinced that the project would be profitable and they would also require the comfort of knowing that long term sales contracts had been entered into for the bulk of the mine output.

28. Thus the marketing and financial aspects have a large degree of interdependence. In fact, the partners expected that some limited financial backing by customers might well be necessary. Bearing in mind that the output is a commodity subject to considerable price fluctuation, this could take the form of back up loan finance in the event that prices were at a lower than expected level in the early years of the mine.

29. The equity needed would be approximately $300 million each from Panama and RTZ. In addition to its equity in the mine, Panama would also have to provide some infrastructure.

30. The money that Panama would need to find would be a very significant increase in its external debt and it is likely that Panama would seek to raise some of this money from such international agencies as the World Bank. Thus the project would be subject to the scrutiny of that august body.

31. The provision of finance was seen as a major task and the terms on which it was available would be critical to the decision to proceed to full construction.

The Impact on Panama

32. Clearly Panama would not embark on a project of this size unless it foresaw clear and substantial benefits to its people and its economy. This issue will not be discussed here - it is taken for granted that the project would not proceed unless this were the case. Indeed, it is the major reason why the project is currently on care and maintenance.

33. The topic that will be discussed is the short term impact that the project would have on Panama before and during the construction phase. There are two major reasons why this would have to be addressed. The first is the size of the project relative to Panama and the second is that Panama does not have any experience of large scale mining.

34. The estimated out-turn cost of the project is some $2 billion; this makes it a large project by any standards. In 1980, the Gross Domestic Project of Panama was some $3.4 billion. The total capital cost of the project would be equivalent to at least 50% of Panama's GDP. Thus its size relative to Panama is much greater than the relative size of the UK North Sea Oil developments compared to the size of the UK's GDP. In addition, the project would require some 80MW of electric power - this is equivalent to about 20-25% of present Panamanian demand. Such an increase would require additional power facilities - almost

certainly hydro-electric, to be constructed in parallel with the mine.

35. Of course, not all the money would be spent in Panama and thus impact directly upon its economy but it was estimated that during the construction period, the GDP of Panama would grow at some 10 to 15 percentage points more than it would have grown without the project.

36. This is an economic boom by any definition and the Panamanian Government was keenly aware that there would have to be careful management to ensure that the possible adverse effects, such as induced inflation, would be minimized.

37. During the second half of the construction period, interest charges on the outstanding loans would be accruing at around $2 million per week. Therefore any delays would prove very expensive.

38. For example, the equipment and materials required to construct the mine and its facilities would cost some $500m in today's values. Most of this would have to be imported into Panama, and would represent a significant additional flow of imports.

39. It was very important that the equipment and materials moved through customs as efficiently as possible so as to minimise any additional costs due to delay.

40. A solution was suggested by the Panamian Government whereby a special unit would be set up responsible solely for dealing with the people, equipment and material arriving in the country and destined for the Project. Project imports and people would have a distinguishing feature in their documentation which would cause them to be dealt with by the special unit rather than the normal customs and immigration facilities. This process was called "one-stop shopping" and it was intended that it be tested during the detailed engineering and pilot plant phase of the project so that an efficient operating system could be in place before construction started.

41. A second major impact upon Panama was foreseen and this is that Panama has no experience of large scale mining. There is a small amount of quarrying and a few very small mines but nothing even approaching the scale of Cerro Colorado. There are several important consequences which it was recognised would have to be solved before major works could commence.

42. An extensive training programme would have to be undertaken so that the maximum number of local people could be employed during the construction and operation of the mines.

43. Panama has a highly developed and sophisticated legal framework covering economic activities in the country. But this framework does not specifically cover large scale mining. An example of this is the lack of detailed environomental

legislation and of health and safety regulations which are specific to mining.

44. A further example is that although Panama has extensive labour laws, these do not cover the specialised requirements of mining which has to be conducted 24 hours a day, 365 days a year.

45. This is not meant to be a criticism but merely reflects that large new developments in any country usually requires a body of new legislation, rules and regulations to be set up. An example of this is the large body of legislation that is now in place here in the UK for offshore oil and gas developments.

Environmental Considerations

46.   The primary environmental considerations of developing any low grade deposit by open cast mining can be simply stated.   It is essentially an earth and rock moving exercise on a large scale.   For Cerro Colorado, some 85 million tonnes of overburden would have to be moved in order to expose the ore body. This amount of material would cover an area of one square kilometre to a depth of around 30 metres.

47. During a typical operating year, some 40 million tonnes of material would be mined of which some 16.5 million tonnes would be processed through the mill and concentrator to produce some 480,000 tonnes of copper concentrates.   Thus out of the   40 million tonnes which were originally mined, only about   0.5 million tonnes would leave Panama.   The remaining 39.5 million tonnes would remain and have to be disposed of safely and in locations where any adverse effects are minimised.   The present indications are that some 200 hectares of steep valley will eventually be covered by waste rock and overburden.

48. It is not possible to move this amount of material on a continuous basis without altering the area around the mine.   The problems are compounded at Cerro Colorado by it being located in a mountainous area of high seasonal rainfall and in the head waters of a river - the San Felix.   The aim must be to minimise any adverse environmental consequences as much as is economically practicable.

49. The environmental studies on developing Cerro Colorado started in 1977 and were carried out under the direction of the Colorado School of Mines Research Institute.   This work is continuing during the present care and maintenance albeit on a reduced level.   The aim of these studies is to establish base line environmental data so as to reliably establish the state of the environment before mining to give a basis against which the effects of mining can be evaluated.

50. This information can be used to decide whether or not the environmental impact is acceptable before the decision to proceed with construction is taken and to monitor the effects of mining during the operations.

51. The studies to date have been undertaken in the immediate area of the orebody, the San Felix river and the Gulf of Chiriqui in the area of the mouth of the San Felix.

52. The activities undertaken as part of these studies have included:

- surface hydrology in the area of the mine site

- stream guaging and water quality monitoring in the rivers and streams in the vicinity of the mine site.

- a preliminary oceanographic study of the Gulf of Chiriqui.

- Marine biology in the Gulf of Chiriqui

- Marine life in the San Felix and its estuary

- studies on the revegetation of tailings

- surveys of fauna species in the mine area

- collection of meteorological data

53. Certain major decisions regarding operating philosophy were taken at an early stage. These can be summarised as :

a) There would be no intentional discharge of any solids or effluents into any river system and,

b) The disposal of waste rock and tailings would be in areas and contained in such a manner as to minimise loss from the dumps into rivers and to be safe in the event of seismic activity.

54. This resulted in plans to dispose of waste ore in suitable valleys and restrained if necessary by dams. A particular problem was the disposal of tailings from the concentrator in a manner which complied with the operating philosophy outlined above.

55. These tailings are a finely divided material which is particularly prone to slumping. It was decided that disposal in the hills constituted an unacceptable risk and thus the plans called for them to be moved to the coast by pipeline. There they would either be stored in the mangrove swamps at the coast or pipelined out to deep water. The final choice would be made following further detailed studies during the pilot plant phase.

56. It is interesting to realise that the capital costs consequent upon this environmental operating philosophy were around 20% of the total capital costs of the project.

57. The major unsolved problem at the present time concerns the effect the mining would have on the San Felix river. At present the river contains large amounts of suspended solids during the rainy season due to natural erosion. However, during

the dry season, the river runs clear and is an important local source of fish and drinking water.

58.   The present studies indicate that it may not be possible to guarantee the dry season use of the river and a major part of the environmental studies during the pilot plant phase would be to investigate ways in which the dry season uses could be preserved. The fall back position, should the river remain cloudy all year round, would be to provide drinking water from other sources such as wells or pipelines.

59.   Although much more work would be done during the pilot plant phase of the studies, the present conclusions of external advisors as well as those of Codemin and RTZ is that there are unlikely to be any serious adverse effects to the environment caused by developing Cerro Colorado.   This is fortunate because open pit mines are like other large natural resource projects in that they cannot be moved.   If the environmental consequences of building a factory, chemical plant, power station, airport, etc. are unacceptable in a particular area, it may well be possible to move the development to a more suitable location.   Ore bodies are where nature has decided – they cannot be moved and if they cannot be developed in a manner which is environmentally acceptable then they cannot be developed.

Sociological Considerations

60.   A project such as Cerro Colorado not only affects the environment, it also affects people and it is more important that any adverse sociological consequences are minimised and any beneficial effects are maximised.

61.   It is true to say that a project of this size would affect everyone in Panama through its impact on gross domestic product, employment and the economy in general. However, the issues that will be discussed in this section are not as wide ranging and are much more concerned with effect on people living close to the mine site and other areas that will directly be affected by the project.

62.   The mine site is located in a sparsely populated part of Panama on land which is of poor agricultural value. The number of people who would be directly affected in that they are living on or close to land that would be utilised by mining and associated operations is around 1500 in some eleven communities.

63.   These people are predominantly the Guaymi who are the most numerous of the indigenous inhabitants who pre-date the colonisation of Panama by the Spanish following the discovering of the Americas in the fifteenth century.

64.   It is estimated that approximately 100,000 such people live in Panama – some 5.5% of the total population.   The Guaymi number between 50,000 and 60,000 and live in the western regions of Panama.

65. The total population of eastern Chiriqui - where the mine site is located - is some 53,000 of whom approximately 32,000 are Guaymi.

66. The Guaymi are a subsistence, agricultural society who have practised "slash and burn" agriculture for many hundreds of years. The soil in the region is very poor and most of the nutrients reside in the foliage and plants. The Guaymi cut down and burn the vegetation to fertilise the soil, plant their crops and move to a new region when the soil is depleted. Agriculturalists have said that this method is successful if the slash and burn cycles are at least twelve years. Thus although the land appears sparsely populated, a very large area is required to support the people.

67. Over recent years the plight of the Guaymi has deteriorated greatly. Their numbers have increased and their lands have been squeezed by cattle ranching. At the moment they have a much lower life expenctancy than that of Panamanians in general, the infant mortality rate is around 25% and malnutrition and tuberculosis are rife.

68. The loss of any of their land is a serious matter for the Guaymi and this is compounded by the mine site being in the area called a "Comarca". This is an area claimed by the Guaymi as being theirs by right and is to be protected from encroachment by non-Guaymi people.

69. This desire is not aimed specifically at the Cerro Colorado project on which the Guaymi feelings are mixed. Some see mining in the area as a development which would seriously and adversely affect their culture. Others see it as an opportunity which would help benefit their precarious existence by the provision of educational, health and welfare facilities as well as jobs.

70. The overall aims of RTZ and Codemin regarding the Guaymi can be summarised as follows:

- the Guaymi would be kept informed of the development of the project so that they understand what is happening and can be involved and take a part in the plans.

- compensation would be given either in cash and/or land to those people displaced by mining operations. The levels of compensation would be discussed and agreed with the Guaymi.

- the Guaymi would be encouraged to seek employment at the mine if they so wished and suitable training would be given to them. The working practices would be sufficiently flexible so as to allow a gradual transition from the traditional seasonal agriocultural pattern of the Guaymi.

- it is proposed to set up a Guaymi Foundation which would

be funded by the mine. The Foundation would help in a better understanding and protection of Guaymi cultural and social values as well as to promote their economic well-being. The precise role of the Foundation would be agreed with the Guaymi and could include agricultural projects, health, education and co-operative businesses for example.

- the present plans envisage that living accommodation for non-Guaymi people working at the mine would be located well outside the Comarca. This causes other problems in that the non-Guaymi workforce would have a long daily journey to and from their homes.

71. A complete sociological study to assess the effects of the project on the local people is planned for the next stage of studies. However, a considerable amount of work has already been done in collecting information and understanding the needs and problems of the local people. This has not been easy because the Guaymi do not have much formal representation unlike other indigenous groups in Panama. Also, for obvious reasons it is difficult for them to imagine the size and implications of a major mine development.

72. The nearest large community to the mine site is called Chami. Its population grew rapidly during the last studies to around 350 Guaymi who were attracted by the easier access and services and social workers provided by the project. Some 40 Guaymi were employed at the mine site during the last work programme.

73. An example of the work carried out by social workers employed by the project was the introduction of new and less land-intensive farming techniques. This resulted in a small pilot vegetable farm near Chami which was run by the community.

74. In conclusion, it is hoped that the Guaymi would grasp the economic and other benefits that the mine would make available to them whilst preserving their own social and cultural values and identity.

CONCLUSIONS

75. The aim of this all too brief paper has been to examine the non-technical aspects of a project such as Cerro Colorado. Each major project is unique and will face its own particular problems; but many of the aspects of Cerro Colorado have parallels elsewhere.

76. Perhaps the most important point is that there must be very close co-operation between all of the disciplines involved in major projects especially during the planning phase. Without this, it is difficult to ensure that such projects are not only technically sound and profitable but also accepted and enjoyed by the local community.

Discussion on Papers 14–16

Introduction to Paper 14 by Mr P.D.V. Marsh

In this introduction to my Paper about the Dubai Project, I want to concentrate on the things which really matter; the lessons which we can learn and hopefully apply to other Projects in the future.

1. Distinguishing between contractor and promoter

Major projects are not always conceived by governments or by already existing client operating organisations. They are sometimes the brain-child of a gifted entrepreneur who, foreseeing a need and the existence of the right blend of ingredients to make his dreams come true, starts the project creation process. He is, however, usually lacking the vehicle by means of which he can follow through that process. He often lacks funds and the necessary technical back-up to support his case. Therefore, he or his organisation turn to a contractor, inviting the latter to become a partner with him in the speculation.

Occasionally it may even be that the contractor himself produces the brain-child. In either event, the result is the same. The contractor becomes part of the promotional set-up – may indeed be at the heart of it – yet the contractor will not as a rule be looking for any major part of his return from being an equity investor. Indeed, often quite the reverse. To be persuaded to put up equity at all, he will have to be convinced that there is no alternative way in which he can stay with the project.

The contractor will expect to earn his money by doing what he knows best, namely, being a contractor. But at some stage, this is going to put him on the other side of the table from the promoter or that part of the promotional organisation which will mutate into a client.

While one can see the contractor in some form of management role, working with the promoter and client-to-be, the conflict of interest situation must become acute if the contractor seeks to secure a negotiated position as the actual builder.

2. The need for an effective client organisation

With promotional projects there is usually no ready-made

client. One has to be created from those who are acting as
promoters and the initial equity investors. Organisations do
not, however, spring into existence overnight. They usually
have a significant gestation period while key staff are
recruited.

Unless, however, the client organisation with its key
permanent staff is there in place when the major construction
contracts are placed, there are bound to be difficulties at a
later stage. If the client is initially a weak relative, say,
to the contractor/s who has/have been involved in the
promotion, then the contracts placed may not be to the
client's advantage. Nor may decisions made at that time
reflect the client's future intentions or operating policies.
As a result, conflict will arise as the client grows in
strength and independence. Changes may need to be negotiated
which can cause confusion and delay. A simple example may be
the client's policy to purchase his initial requirement of
spares through the main contractor, or direct; and if the
latter, what information will he require.

3. Minimising the number of consultants

I believe there probably exists a law to the effect that the
time taken to reach any decision varies as to the cube of the
numbers of differing parties involved. Certainly it is the
case that any client receiving advice from two or more
advisers, each having their own individual approach to the
issue involved, and each often having their own personal
position to protect, is placed in a difficult situation.
Which advice does he prefer and, if challenged, perhaps by
auditors, how is he to justify accepting one and rejecting the
other? It encourages the client to develop his own
organisation.

One area of particular difficulty relates to the respective
roles of the engineer and the quantity surveyor. In theory,
the quantity surveyor is there to provide a service to the
engineer on matters relating to monthly valuations, and to
prepare the certificate for approval and signature by the
engineer. Unfortunately, if the quantity surveyor is at the
same time acting as the overall cost consultant to the client,
there can develop a strong direct relationship between the
quantity surveyor and the client, which progressively erodes
the independent position of the engineer.

Ideally, in my view, the client should have one professional
adviser - the consulting engineer - appointed as the engineer
under the contract, who would be responsible for obtaining
such assistance as he might require on specialist matters.

4. Levels of management

As a result of the method of financing and the recourse
requirements of ECGD, it was necessary to sub-let the work,
particularly on the mechanical and electrical side, in large
packages.

186

However, this did give rise to certain problems because the sub-sub-contractors were, in particular cases, major firms in their own right, with particular expertise, who had necessarily to be involved in technical and commercial decision-making related to their scope of work. They also had, outside the contract, direct relationships with the client.

While splitting up a major package into, say, three component parts, clearly increases the main contractor's risk and interface responsibilities, it also makes for more rapid decision-making. It also avoids the temptation of going direct and thereby breaking the contractual chain.

5. The project to be right

Any major project costing in excess of a billion dollars and which is conceived, designed and built over five or so years, will be exposed to shocks. Inflation can play havoc with budgets. Markets and selling prices for the product can dramatically alter. Political support can fade; the policies of governments change. New or improved technologies can arise. Accidental disaster can strike.

If such a project is to survive these kinds of shocks, it must, from the outset, be fundamentally right for the country concerned; not be just marginally so, or only if particularly favourable conditions exist. If at the conception stage, one finds oneself engaging in the gentle art of special pleading, then be warned.

The Dubai smelter was right for three basic reasons. First, the availability and price of gas; second, the production of drinking water which on any prediction Dubai was going to need; and third, the plant, with its minimum labour force requirement, its location next to a port and environmental cleanliness, fitted into the Dubai long-term social and economic development plans.

MR D. DENSON, W.A. Fairhurst & Partners

We are currently involved with the London Docklands Development Corporation, itself a major international project in view of the site area of eight square miles; a time for completion of ten years; and a contract value of some £500m; with the international status being acquired by the number of overseas investors.

From this background, and being concerned with all aspects of a project, I was very interested to see the subject of quality assurance raised - probably for the first time in this Conference - in Mr Weatherseed's slide of site organisation.

My understanding of quality assurance is that it is the system which ensures quality; and that quality control is the implementation of that system. Quality control is as old as civil engineering itself, but quality assurance is a relatively new discipline. It was probably started in the American missile industry, where on account of the complex nature of the project, various component parts were manufactured at different locations across the country.

When the parts were due to come together for assembly, it was sometimes the case that certain parts did not arrive to programme; or when they did arrive they did not fit together; or if they did fit, then in some instances they malfunctioned on test. This was clearly unacceptable and, as a consequence, the engineers designed systems to prevent these costly errors from occurring, and quality assurance was born.

One of the prime requirements of quality assurance is that it must be completely independent of day-to-day contract pressures. In the site organisation diagram, this did not appear to be the case, as the Quality Assurance Manager was reporting directly to the Project Manager.

A benefit of quality assurance is that the system is thought to be cost- effective, as additional personnel costs are offset by the need to undertake operations only once.

To summarise, can I ask Mr Weatherseed whether the quality assurance system was truly independent of everyday contract pressures; whether the system was found to be cost-effective; and whether quality assurance was a part of McAlpine's normal site working arrangements, or had the system been imposed by the client?

MR WEATHERSEED

The application of quality assurance was one of the conditions of the contract, and the system was based on the client's requirement.

McAlpine have always practised strong quality control systems and the company have written procedures covering many aspects of the work that a contractor meets during the course of a contract. This was the first contract for the company on which quality assurance was experienced, which meant that our procedures had to be formalised, and personnel trained to carry out this new management discipline.

The Quality Assurance Manager and his team were an independent section and were not in any way involved with the progress of the work. The former was directly responsible to the Project Manager who was the company's senior representative on site, whereas the Agent was responsible for the everyday running of the contract.

The quality assurance team's role was to ensure that quality assurance was being carried out, not only by McAlpine but also to ensure that the latter's sub-contractors were meeting their obligations too.

With regard to the apparent cost-effectiveness of quality assurance, it is impossible to prove or refute this. Quality assurance does cost money, as additional staff are required not only to apply it but to administer as well, particularly in view of all the paperwork that is generated. Like everything in life, there are good and bad parts — and quality assurance is no exception.